Diamonds in the Rough

Diamonds in the Rough

Dr. Lee Roberson

SWORD of the LORD PUBLISHERS

P. O. BOX 1099, MURFREESBORO, TN 37133

Printed and Bound in the United States of America

DEDICATION

I dedicate this second volume of illustrations to two very special people: to my wife, Mrs. Caroline Allen Roberson, for fifty-nine years of loyal, consistent and consecrated service for Christ at my side; and to my secretary, Mrs. Gloria Shadowens, for her dedication to Christ and for her faithfulness in the work of our Lord. She had a definite part in this book by typing, proofreading and preparation of the material for printing.

Lee Roberson

CONTENTS

PREFACE

In a few days I will come to my 88th birthday. I pause daily to give thanks to God for saving me, calling me and guiding me. It has been a long road but a very happy and blessed one. There have been heartaches, disappointments and sorrows; but in it all I have known the presence of God, the peace of God, and the power of God.

I rejoice in the thousands who have come to an acceptance of Christ through these years. I rejoice that I have had the joy and privilege of baptizing many thousands in the churches where I have pastored—Germantown, Tennessee; Greenbrier, Tennessee; Fairfield, Alabama; and forty years and six months at the great Highland Park Baptist Church in Chattanooga, Tennessee.

The illustrations in this book are taken from the sermons I have preached in the past sixty-seven years.

Lee Roberson
April 3, 1997

BIBLE

HOW HE STUDIED THE BIBLE

One great Bible teacher said his method was simply to sit down with his Bible and begin reading. As he read, he took notes with pencil and paper. Then when he finished his reading, he wrote out a brief outline of what he had just read.

He stated also that he would, after reading of the Word of God, ask himself, *What practical application can I make of these truths to my own life this day?*

This is an example that we must not ignore. Read much from God's holy Word.

●●●●

THE PLACE OF THE BIBLE IN OUR LIVES

Neglect of the Word of God brings loss of power. George Mueller said, "The first three years after my conversion I neglected the Word of God. Since I began to search it diligently, the blessing has been wonderful. I have read the Bible through one hundred times and always with increasing delight."

Mr. Mueller went on to tell his story. He was pastor of a church of 1,200 believers; he cared for five immense orphanages; he answered thousands of letters by hand; he had a publishing depot and other heavy responsibilities. He said, "The vigor of our spiritual life will be in exact proportion to the place held by the Word in our lives and thoughts."

●●●●

THE SINGLE BOOK WORTH SAVING!

Alexander Duff, the great missionary, sailed for India on the *Lady Holland*. His clothes, his prized possessions and his library of eight hundred volumes were all on board.

Within a few miles of India, a shipwreck occurred. The passengers were saved, but their possessions went down to the bottom of the sea. On the seashore, Alexander Duff looked out to the sea, hoping against hope that some of his possessions might have cast upon the shore.

Then some passengers saw something—something small—floating on top of the water. Nearer and nearer it came while anxious eyes watched. What could it be? The missionary waded into the water, got hold of the floating object and returned. It was the Bible!

Of all his books and possessions, that single Book was saved! Mr. Duff took it to mean that this one rescued Book was worth more than all his other books and possessions.

Heartened, Alexander Duff began his career as a missionary in India. Reading from the Bible, he conducted his first class—a group of five boys meeting under a banyan tree. A week later the class had grown to three hundred listeners.

Many applications can be made from this story.

••••

DR. KELLY'S PRESCRIPTION

A woman of nervous temperament visited the world-renowned physician, Dr. Howard A. Kelly of Johns Hopkins. The cares of life threatened her physical strength, even her reasoning. Having given her symptoms to the physician, she was greatly astonished at his prescription:

"Madam, what you need is to read the Bible more!"

"But, Doctor...," began the bewildered woman.

"Go home and read your Bible an hour a day," the great

man reiterated with kindly authority, "then come back to see me a month from today."

At first the woman was inclined to become angry, but she reflected with a pang of conscience that she had neglected the daily reading of God's Word and "the secret places of the most High," where formerly she communed with her Lord.

In coming back to her God and His Word, the joys of her salvation returned. When she came back to the doctor a month later, he said, "Well, I see you have been an obedient patient. Do you feel as if you need any other medicine now?"

"No, Doctor, I am a different person. But how did you know what I needed?"

Taking up his worn and well-marked Bible, he said, "If I omit my daily reading of God's Word, I not only lose my joy, but I lose my greatest source of strength and skill. Your case called not for medicine but for a source of peace and strength outside your own self. My prescription, when tried, works wonders!"

••••

CONVICTED BY A SCRIPTURE

An unsaved student in a university was having breakfast in the home of one of his college friends. He talked freely with a friend's mother about his ambitions to become a lawyer, to advance in the political world, to acquire fame and fortune, and to become wealthy.

The soul-minded mother in that home was quiet and thoughtful while he talked.

Upon leaving, as the student shook hands with the mother, she put a note in his hand but didn't say a word. He put it in his pocket.

In the privacy of his own room in the college dormitory, he opened it and read, "For what is a man profited, if he shall gain the whole world, and lose his own soul?" (Matt. 16:26).

The truth of that verse pierced his heart like a sharp sword. Conviction for sin and conversion to Christ were the results.

It is the Word of God that gives a heart-passion for souls and brings conviction to the lost.

••••

A GIFT NO GOOD UNLESS RECEIVED

The wise attitude to take toward the gift of everlasting life is to repent, believe and receive it.

A poor man fell heir to an antique desk of which he was very proud. This beautiful and valuable piece of furniture added much charm to his home.

He had possession of this desk for years before he began making practical use of it. One day he discovered a secret drawer. In the drawer was a jewel case full of sparkling gems. What wealth and delight were his for the discovery!

Our city is filled with churches. Bibles by the thousands are found in homes, but a gift will do no good unless one receives it.

Christ stands ready to give everlasting life to those who will receive it.

••••

TIME FOR THE WORLD; NO
TIME FOR THE WORD

Recently, I visited a lady in one of our hospitals in Chattanooga. She said she was a Christian. In her hands was a worldly magazine, another was stuffed under her pillow, and one was on the table beside her bed. The cigarettes were there by her side.

I said, "And where is your Bible?"

"Oh, I forgot it when I came to the hospital."

I asked, "Then why don't you read the Gideon Bible on the table beside your bed?"

"Oh, I didn't know there was one."

She had plenty of time for the filth of the world but no time to find the answers for her life.

• • • •

NEW GLORY ADDED TO "OLD GLORY"

Peter Marshall, once chaplain of the U. S. Senate, wisely said, "It is time we put the Bible back into our government, and time for our statesmen to make their decisions on all moral questions on the basis of the authority of God's holy Word. It is only by applying Christ's solutions to the problems that plague us, and it is only by living under His blessing and guidance, that we can ever hope to add any new glory to Old Glory."

• • • •

PAUL'S POSSESSIVE PRONOUN

While reading the little book of Philippians, I began to underscore Paul's possessive pronoun:

"My God" 1:3; 4:19
"My heart" 1:7
"My record" 1:8
"My bonds" 1:13
"My salvation" 1:19
"My hope" 1:20
"My body" 1:20
"My labour" 1:22
"My joy" 2:2; 4:1
"My beloved" 2:12
"My brother" 2:25
"My wants" 2:25
"My Lord" 3:8
"My fellow labourers" 4:3

What a list! What Paul had, I can have because he said by inspiration to the Corinthians, "All things are your's." Paul did not say that he was the sole owner of all things. He was the possessor of much by claim. It was offered to him, and he received it.

••••

MAC ARTHUR READS THE WORD

Major General Courtney Whitney wrote a biography of General Douglas MacArthur. In the story, he tells of a night when he was called in before the general. They were facing a big battle.

The general was having some difficulty making up his mind whether to enter into the battle at once or to wait a few hours.

Major General Whitney came to the general's bedroom and found the general in bathrobe and slippers pacing the floor. Whitney was told to be seated, and General MacArthur, in a kind of self-debate, began to talk as he paced the floor, reviewing one by one the arguments against the proposed landing in the morning. MacArthur countered with reasons for the surprised assault until finally, at about 2:30 a.m., he concluded his soliloquy with the statement that he felt certain that his decision had been a sound one whose hazards had to be accepted. The general turned to Major General Whitney and said, "Thanks, Court, thanks for listening to me. Now let's get some sleep."

Then the Major General added these words, "He [General MacArthur] threw off his robe, climbed into his bed, and reached to the table alongside to pick up his Bible."

Does not this single statement partially account for the greatness of General MacArthur? He could have picked up Virgil or Shakespeare or Bunyan or Keats or Milton or Emerson, but he did not. He picked up the Word of God.

This is the Book that comforts and challenges. This is the Book that gives light to our pathway. This is the Book that strengthens us in our hour of weakness. This is the Book that gives light in the place of darkness. This is the Book that gives food for the soul and refreshment for the heart.

••••

"AS LONG AS YOU DON'T USE IT, YOU DON'T NEED IT"

Some people spend so much time reading books about how to read the Bible that they never actually get around to reading the Bible. Unless you read your Bible, what point is there in having one?

An illustration of this comes from the front page of one of our newspapers. The driver of a big truck cut in front of a compact car without giving a signal. A little farther on, both had to stop at a red light.

The driver of the compact car got out, took a car wrench, marched straight to the truck, and smashed the rearview mirror. He looked at the driver and announced, "As long as you don't use it, you don't need it!" Then he turned, went back to his car and drove off.

The truck driver's response was simply this: "I deserved it."

What good is the Bible to you if you keep it closed?

••••

SHE EXPERIENCED "SOUTHERN EMOTIONALISM"

Curious to see something of the "southern emotionalism," a young lady from the North came to hear a man preach while in a southern college town. While there she began to experience it herself. Her heart was touched. She realized that she was neglecting God in her life.

She went to talk with the pastor. The conversation

revealed that she knew no more about the Bible than if she had been reared in a pagan land.

The pastor placed his Bible in her hands and asked her to read Isaiah 53:4, 5, substituting the singular personal pronoun for the plural. So she read, 'Surely He hath borne *my* griefs, and carried *my* sorrows: yet *I* did esteem Him stricken, smitten of God, and afflicted. But He was wounded for *my* transgressions, He was bruised for *my* iniquities, the chastisement of *my* peace was upon Him, and with His stripes *I* am healed.'

The sword went straight to her heart. "Do you mean that Jesus did that for me?"

Of course he told her yes and further explained to her the blessed Good News.

In a short time she happily surrendered to the Lord and accepted Him as her Saviour. Now she began to rejoice in Him.

When she saw the pastor again, she said, "I can hardly wait until I get home! I have a brother there who has never heard that story."

••••

DON'T MISS THE BEAUTY OF HIS WORD

One evening Lorado Taft, the sculptor, called some of his friends to the porch of his summer home to see a beautiful sunset. The western sky was a fairyland of shifting shapes and colors. As the group marveled at the beauty of it, Mr. Taft spoke in such vivid language and so interestingly that his guests began to see the sunset through *his* eyes.

All the while, the maid who served them refreshments was standing by unnoticed. Suddenly she asked, "Mr. Taft, may I run home for a minute?"

"What do you want at your home at this particular moment?" he inquired.

"I want to show Mother the sunset!"

"But your mother has lived here a good many years; surely she must have seen many sunsets."

"Oh, no," came the earnest reply. "We never saw the sunset here until you came."

Quite often we read the Word of God but fail to get the significance of what God is saying. We miss the beauty of His Word. We miss seeing it with our own eyes. We miss also our obligations to the One who created such beauty for us to enjoy.

COMPASSION

A CHILD'S CONCERN FOR HER LOST BROTHER

Dr. George W. Truett told about a Sunday morning service when a little foreign girl accepted Jesus Christ as Saviour. (She spoke English but in a broken way.) When she came forward, Dr. Truett tried to talk to her but could not understand what she was saying. "If you don't mind, I will talk to you after the service," he said. Then he turned away to deal with others.

When he looked back, the little girl had her head bowed and was crying. He went back to her and said, "Don't cry, my dear. I will talk with you after the service. I feel sure that you are saved, but I would like to talk with you in private."

The child answered, "Sir, I'm not crying about that. I know Jesus has saved my soul, but my brother is lost and will be going to Hell. I want to see him saved."

Dr. Truett had no hesitation in presenting her name to the church. He felt sure that she had been saved since she manifested such concern for her brother.

••••

GOD CARES WHEN A BABY DIES!

This is a strange and impersonal world. People don't care much anymore. There is little compassion about us.

I was reading the other day about Henry Grady, the great southern statesman. While living in the North with his family, they lost a child. Mr. Grady said to his wife, "Let's go back home where people care when a baby dies."

The world doesn't care much for us or our problems, but I have great news for you—I know God cares!

● ● ● ●

THANK GOD FOR SOUL-WINNING SUNDAY SCHOOL TEACHERS!

Sunday school teachers should be concerned for those in their charge. On page one of a book on evangelism, I read this:

A twelve-year-old boy stood to give his testimony at a midweek service in the Addison Street Baptist Church in Chicago.

"One year ago," he said, "a man knocked at our door and asked if there was anyone in our house who didn't attend church that he could invite to church and Sunday school.

"I told him I had never been to a church but would like to go. The next Sunday, someone came and walked me to church.

"One year ago I didn't know there was a God or that He had a Son named Jesus. One year ago I didn't know that I was a sinner or that Jesus was my Saviour. One year ago I hadn't ever seen a Bible, but for the past year I have been in Mr. Berriman's class. He gave me a Bible and taught me about God, and he taught me how to take Jesus as my personal Saviour. I accepted Jesus Christ, and now my heart is different."

Thank God for Sunday school teachers who engage in the major business of winning souls. God pity the poor Sunday school teacher who fails to have a concern for others.

● ● ● ●

DRY EYES AND EMPTY ALTARS

I read this statement a few days ago: "Dry eyes and empty altars seem to have lost their stigma; no longer do they disturb the great majority of believers."

This is quite true. Our churches are filled with those who never shed one tear over a lost world. Our altars are quite often empty. No compassionate, praying people are there getting themselves closer to God and crying out for the salvation of souls.

•••••

UNTOUCHED BY THE LOSTNESS OF MEN

Many years ago the janitor of a church in Chicago came into the church study to find out why the preacher, Dr. Frank Gonzales, was not in his pulpit. It was already five minutes past the time for the service to begin.

He found the great pastor at his desk, looking out over the rooftops of the slum area of the city with tears in his eyes.

"Pastor, it's time for you to preach," the sexton told him.

"Thank you for reminding me. I had forgotten the time."

"But why the tears?" the sexton asked.

"I have been sitting here looking at those houses in the slums. Aren't they terrible? Life must be horrible for those desperate people."

"Yes, I know," said the sexton. "It is hard, but don't worry about it, Sir. You'll get used to it."

"I know," replied the pastor. "That's why the tears."

Oh, the tragic truth of such an illustration! We get used to the fact that people are lost and dying and going to Hell. We are untouched by the tragedy of the lostness of men.

•••••

NO COMPASSION FOR CHILDREN

Some years ago when we first began this work, the bus children came rushing into the church. Some were not so clean. One usher straightened himself up big and tall and said, "If you're going to have a church for the riffraff, count me out. I'm leaving."

He left, and no one asked him to return. He showed us that he had not the Spirit of the Lord Jesus Christ about children.

••••

"O SIR, NOT SHE, BUT ME!"

Dr. H. A. Ironside told about one of the generals of Cyrus the Great, king of Persia.

When the general came home from a campaign, he was shocked to find that in his absence his wife had been arrested and was in prison, charged with treachery against her country. The trial was to be held that very day.

The general hastened to the court of Cyrus. The guards brought in his own beloved wife. This poor woman, pale and anxious, tried to answer the charges brought against her but to no avail.

Her husband, standing near, heard the stern voice of the Persian ruler pronounce the death sentence. As they were about to drag her out to behead her, he ran forward and threw himself down at the feet of the emperor.

"O Sir," he cried, "not she, but me. I will give my life for hers. Put me to death, but spare my wife."

As Cyrus looked on, so touched was he by the general's deep devotion and love for his wife that his heart was softened. He remembered too how faithful this one had been; so he gave the command to let the wife go free. She was fully pardoned.

As her husband led her out of the room, he said, "Did you

notice the kind look in the eyes of the emperor as he pronounced the word of pardon?"

She replied, "I did not see the face of the emperor. The only face that I could see was that of the man who was willing to die for me."

One day we shall stand before the Son of God and see the One who died for us. "Christ died for our sins according to the scriptures" (I Cor. 15:3).

CONVICTIONS

MEN ARE MOVED BY MEN OF CONVICTIONS

A few days ago, I heard the pastor of the First Baptist Church of a large city speak on TV. Not one time did he mention Jesus Christ in his lengthy message.

As he closed his sermon with prayer, I thought that surely he would mention the name of Christ; but no, he omitted the name altogether.

I am quite aware of what happened. Doubtless, someone told him that it would be better if he didn't mention the name of Christ on television. Then he would not offend people!

Let your convictions be strong, for the world can be moved by men of convictions.

••••

CONVICTIONS—WE MUST HAVE THEM

Convictions—yes, we must have them!

I was reading about Winston Churchill, a great leader of England in times of crisis. Strangely, Mr. Churchill had few spiritual beliefs. He rarely went to church, and he gave almost no expression of his convictions regarding spiritual truth.

There are those who would say, "Well, if Churchill didn't believe, then why should I?"

O my friend, whether or not anyone else believes, known or unknown, I must believe what God has told me in this

Book. My convictions must be based on this Bible, the Word of God.

•••

CONVICTIONS MEAN LITTLE UNLESS YOU SHOW THEM

Between a motel and the restaurant was an unused railroad track. The tracks were yellow with rust. The sidewalk from the motel to the restaurant ran down to the tracks and picked up on the other side. There were no warning gates or signals, for few trains were seen there.

Your convictions mean little unless you use them. Joshua and Caleb knew that Israel could take the Land of Promise. They stated their convictions. As a result of their firm faith in God, they received the blessings of the Lord.

DEATH

LIFE UNCERTAIN

A few days ago I made a call to a funeral home to try to comfort a family. After talking to them, I knelt in prayer and asked God to bless and comfort their hearts.

I went outside and got into my car. Many thoughts began crowding my mind. I took a piece of paper and wrote down a few.

How uncertain life is. I thought of James 4:14: "For what is your life? It is even a vapour, that appeareth for a little time and then vanisheth away."

I thought of how sudden death is. The deceased resting in the casket in the funeral home was sitting in a chair and drinking a glass of water when death suddenly struck her. Water spilled on the floor, but she retained her hold on the glass even when death came.

Are you prepared if death came today or tomorrow? If so, then you have nothing to fear. If not, your next stop is Hell! It need not be. Prepare yourself for eternity!

••••

"I AM DYING LOST!"

Rev. George Cates was pastor in a small town in Texas. When a friend became suddenly and seriously ill, he was called to his friend's bedside.

When Rev. Cates asked, "How is it with your soul?" the friend answered, "George, we've been together a lot. We've hunted and fished; we've talked about many subjects, including religion, churches, your ministry and the Bible; but, George, you have never pressed the matter of my soul's eternal welfare. Now it's too late! I am dying lost!"

Then with an awful, indescribable look in his eyes and an unspeakable wail and pathos in his voice, for the last hour of his life he spoke only one word—"Lost! Lost! Lost!"

We are told that George Cates resigned his church and went into evangelistic work. Receiving a picture of what it means to be lost, he went everywhere telling the story of Jesus Christ and urging sinners to accept Christ now and be saved before death came, for there is no salvation after death.

••••

ABSENT FROM THE BODY, PRESENT WITH HIS LORD

Just a few days ago I conducted a funeral for one of our members, Mr. Jess Peardon, 88 years of age. The family was large—7 children, 35 grandchildren, 53 great-grandchildren, 3 great-great-grandchildren—and he had many friends and other relatives.

When the service was over we drove through the city, around the side of Lookout Mountain, then took the highway heading toward Nashville. As the funeral procession drove along the hills and beside the river between Chattanooga and Jasper, the fog settled down upon us, making it difficult to see even a few feet ahead of each car.

Finally we reached a lonely little country cemetery. The rain was falling, and the mud was thick. At the head of the grave I read from I Corinthians 15, then turned to the old familiar portion, Psalm 23.

Jess Peardon was a saved man. At his death he was "absent from the body...present with the Lord."

Just one out of this great Highland Park Baptist Church, but he was one. God loved him. Jesus saved him.

The fog, the rain, the mud, the sadness of life do not bother this brother now; he is with his Lord.

•••

THE REQUEST OF AN INFIDEL AT DEATH

At the close of the last century the notorious infidel, Robert Ingersoll, died. This man had spent a lifetime attacking Christian beliefs. He played the fool on many occasions. For example, how foolish it was for him to stand before an audience and say, "If there is a God in Heaven, I will give Him five minutes to strike me dead." Our God doesn't need to heed foolish ramblings of man.

Bob Ingersoll died. Notices of the funeral services were sent out, carrying the brief sentence: "There will be no *singing*."

Of course there would be no singing. What could they sing about? Had Ingersoll's contentions been true, there wouldn't be anything facing humanity but blank, naked despair.

(Today singing is omitted at too many funerals. The Christian has a song. Let the words of Christian hymns be used to speak to the hearts of those who are in sorrow.)

•••

DYING COURAGEOUSLY AND WITHOUT FEAR

A few days ago I read a very interesting thing that happened at Emory University. A professor in the school of medicine had passed away. A second-year medical student went to the newspaper office and told the editor, "I don't think you ought to handle Dr. Walker's death with a routine obituary notice. The way he died was the most impressive thing I have seen in the six years I have been at Emory. Everyone is talking about it."

The editor said, "Tell me about it."

The boy told him this story:

> Dr. Walker had Hodgkin's sarcoma for two and one-half years or more. He knew for at least six months that he would not get well, and so did all the students, though he never mentioned it and neither did we.
>
> We sat and watched him waste away, but not even that could keep him from his classes. He dragged himself up there week after week and taught us, dying a little bit every day. He taught us the week before he died.
>
> We began to realize all we were getting in medical school, what it took to give it to us, and how little we were giving. One of the professors said that watching Dr. Walker die the way he did gave us hope that there was enough of the same substance in all men, including himself, to permit us to face death in the same way.
>
> Here is something else. On Sunday night, the night before he died, Dr. Walker walked into Emory Hospital and told an intern, "I've come into the hospital to die." He was gone in less than twenty-four hours.

What had this man done? He showed them how to live courageously. He showed how to die without fear. He was able to demonstrate in an unforgettable manner the way to die.

●●●●

GOD ANSWERED THE CHALLENGE OF AN UNBELIEVER

Lady Anne Grimston didn't believe in life after death. When she lay dying in her palatial home, she said to a friend, "It is as unlikely that I shall live again as that a tree should grow from my body."

She was buried in a marble tomb; the grave was marked

by a large marble slab and surrounded by an iron railing.

Years later the marble slab had moved a little. Then it cracked, and through the crack a small tree grew. The tree continued to grow, tilting the stone and breaking the marble masonry, until today it surrounds the tomb with its roots and it has torn the railing out of the ground with its massive trunks. The tree at Lady Anne's grave is a large one.

That story has been given many times. It bears a weighty lesson. In a churchyard in England stands a great four-trunked tree growing out of a grave.

So it is that God answered the challenge of an unbeliever. That is not the end to it all. She will have to stand before the great white throne and hear her final doom. She will be resurrected—not in a body of glory, but in one of shame and contempt.

••••

"WHAT IF I HAD BEEN DEATH?"

A preacher went to see a man. He told him, "I want to talk to you about your soul's salvation."

"I am too busy to talk right now," the man replied.

The preacher took him by the hand, pulled him down close to himself, and whispered in his ear, *"What if I had been Death?"*

If Death came for you in this hour, would you be ready? This is the time to repent, to believe.

FAITH

HOW TO GROW FAITH

How true it is—fear, anxiety, grief and gloom will disappear when faith takes over.

D. L. Moody said that he prayed for faith and thought it would strike him like lightning; but one day he read the Bible and found these words: "So then faith cometh by hearing, and hearing by the word of God" (Rom. 10:17).

He said, "I had closed my Bible and prayed for faith. Now I am studying my Bible, and faith has been growing ever since."

We conquer by faith!

••••

DEFINITION OF FAITH

Charles Wesley once engaged in a discussion on the subject of faith. No one was able to furnish a satisfactory definition to him or to anyone else present. In the midst of their perplexity, Mr. Wesley said, "Let us call on Mrs. So-and-so," naming an individual of good sense and of very deep piety. "She," continued Wesley, "can tell us just what faith is because she is consciously exercising it."

When asked to tell what faith is, her reply was this: "It is taking God at His word."

Mr. Wesley exclaimed, "That will do!"

••••

THE FAITH OF JUST ONE COUNTS

A missionary said to a native woman, "There is no use to keep the church open any longer. You may as well give me the key."

The little church house had been built in a town where the natives had once professed Christianity but had declined in interest; they had quit attending and had returned to their idols.

The woman to whom the missionary spoke was poor in purse but steadfast in spirit and didn't want to give up the key to the little church.

The missionary added as he looked at her sorrowful face, "There is a place of Christian worship in the village there—only three miles off—and those who really want to serve God can walk that distance!"

The little lady said, "Oh, do not take the key away! I at least will go to the church daily. I will sweep it, trim its lamp, and keep it burning; and I will go on praying. Someday God may hear, and a blessing will come."

The missionary said, "Oh, well, then keep the key."

He went his way.

Some years later when he returned to the village, to his surprise he found the church crowded with repentant sinners. A great harvest of souls had been reaped. The steadfastness of one lady was the secret of the whole success.

••••

"I AM NOW TRUSTING GOD, AND ALL IS WELL"

A lady dietician works at one of our hospitals. She goes to the various sickrooms and checks on the food given the patients.

Her mother became very ill and hovered between life and death for some time. I went to the sickroom and prayed with her. Later she passed away.

A few days ago I again saw the dietician whose mother had died. She said, "I don't know what I'm going to do. I cry all the time. Oh, how I miss my mother!"

Rather sharply I told the dear lady that her faith must be in God, that she must look beyond this life of sorrow to the life ahead. I reminded her that her mother was a Christian and was now in Heaven, that her body was now placed in the grave but her soul was in the presence of God, that her mother is absent from the body and present with the Lord.

I told her that she was showing very poor evidence of her faith in Christ by weeping and worrying all the time.

This past week I saw her again in the hospital. This time she had a smile on her face as she said, "Your sharp words hurt for awhile, but then they helped. I am now trusting God, and all is well."

••••

EXERCISE YOUR FAITH

On one of the South Sea Islands some years ago an explorer found large, heavy birds which had lost their ability to fly. Once flying birds and at home in the air, they now were unable to fly. The explorer wondered why, then set out to discover the reason.

He did not have to work at the task long until he had the answer.

On this island these birds could obtain an abundance of food by merely walking, hopping or jumping a few feet at a time. They had become very heavy and overweight by incessant eating and not using their wings to fly.

Two things emerged from this study: first, the birds had not used their wings for so long a time that they had become shortened, flabby, and unable to bear them up as aforetime; second, the birds had overeaten until their obesity was their own undoing. They were so heavy that no matter how hard they flapped their wings when frightened and needing to fly, they couldn't mount the air.

The story has an illustration for all of us. There is a danger that we will know our Christ, rest upon His promises, understand the meaning and power of faith, but somehow not exercise our faith. We still worry, still fret, but we don't launch out into the deep and use the faith that has been given to us.

FORGIVENESS

LISTEN! JOHN IS SPEAKING!

At the World's Fair in Chicago in the year 1893, a public discussion was held by the representatives of the world's leading religions—Buddhism, Mohammedanism, Shintoism and others. Eloquently and beautifully, they declared the virtues of their particular faiths.

The case for Christianity was presented by Dr. Joseph Cook. In the course of his great address, he turned to those who were seated on the platform, the men who had already spoken, and said, "Gentlemen, I wish to present to you a woman with a great burden. She has committed murder and is tormented by her conscience. She cannot sleep by night. She has been driven to the place of despair. Is there anything in your religion or in your philosophy that will help this woman?"

Then he waited, as though expecting an answer.

After a bit, he went on and said, "You have eloquently spoken, but you have told this poor woman nothing that would help her become free from the burden of her guilt and the stain of her sin."

He went on: "Now we shall ask another." Then Joseph Cook lifted his eyes heavenward and cried, "John, you tell us. You tell this woman how she can find freedom from the guilt of her sin and how she can have peace again."

"Listen!" he said dramatically. "John is speaking: 'The

blood of Jesus Christ his Son cleanseth us from all sin.'"

• • • •

PARDON SIGNED BY THE BLOOD

A minister spoke one Sunday morning to a group of three hundred prisoners. At the end of the service, one of the inmates, with a glowing face, came to him. He could not conceal the ecstacy of his joy. "I am the happiest man in this state today!"

The preacher asked, "Why are you so happy?"

"The governor has pardoned me. He has already signed my pardon papers. At sunrise tomorrow, I will go out through that gate a free man."

Thank God for the time I received the Lord Jesus Christ as my Saviour! My pardon papers were not signed by the president of the United States nor the governor of the state of Kentucky, but signed by the Lord Jesus Christ. They were not signed in some of the fading ink of this world, but signed with the blood of Jesus Christ.

Thank God that I heard the message of the Saviour and received the Lord Jesus Christ!

• • • •

"O GOD, I'M GUILTY!"

Former Governor Pat Neff of Texas spoke to an assembly of convicts in a penitentiary of that state. He finished his speech by stating that he would remain to listen if any man wanted to speak with him. He further announced that what he heard would be held in confidence. "Nothing a man might tell me will be used against you."

When the meeting was over, a large group of men remained. Many were life-termers. One by one told his story to the governor: he was there by a frame-up, an injustice, a judicial blunder or any one of many other reasons. Each asked to be freed.

Finally one man came up and said, "Mr. Governor, I just want to say that I'm guilty. I did what they sent me here for, but I believe I have paid for it. If I were granted the right to go out, I would do everything I could to be a good citizen and prove myself worthy of your mercy."

This man the governor pardoned.

So it must be with the great God who can pardon. The one difference is, we cannot say that we have paid for any of it. We can only come and say, "O God, I just want to say that I am guilty. I am a sinner, a rebel against Thy power and Thy justice, but I believe Jesus Christ paid for my sin."

This is the man whom God pardons. When we see ourselves lost and undone and come to the Lord Jesus Christ and receive the salvation He offers, we have life everlasting.

GIVING

WILL YOU LEAVE CHRIST FORGOTTEN IN A CORNER?

Up in Kentucky a family of about thirty-five, counting children and grandchildren, will assemble after the Christmas Eve service. That is when they give out their Christmas gifts.

This is done in a very unique way and done in the same way year after year. In the living room, the grandfather makes the talk about Christ. He reads from the Bible, never hurrying. The children are impatient, but he ignores them. He reads gently, carefully and lovingly. The family hears again and again the beautiful Christmas story.

After prayer he is ready to give out gifts. This too is done in a certain way and with a certain deliberation. There is no hurry. He enjoys his part, and the family is happy to allow him the privilege.

Just exactly one year ago he began giving out the gifts on Christmas Eve. One by one the names of the children were called: "John," "Joan," "Mary," etc. They responded and came forward to receive the gifts that Grandfather had for them. Each child would thank Grandfather. He called many names, and many gifts were given. Occasionally he would pick up a gift and put it over to one side. No name was called. The gift was untouched.

Last year a little boy about ten sat near the Christmas tree and near his grandfather. There was the tearing of paper, laughing and much good-natured banter; but the little boy near the tree didn't have a single gift, while others had several. All were happy but this one sober lad.

When the grandfather had finished, the boy sat there empty-handed, and big tears began to trickle down his cheeks. He didn't say anything for awhile, then he quietly turned to his grandpa and said, "Granddaddy, don't I get anything?"

The grandfather had been playing a trick on his grandson, but it backfired because of the boy's heartbroken cry, "Granddaddy, don't I get anything?"

My friend, what will Christ get from you? Will you leave Him forgotten in the corner? At Christmas, will you give to others and forget your Saviour?

••••

"LITTLE IS MUCH WHEN GOD IS IN IT"

A few years ago I saw the famous Buckner Orphans' Home in Dallas, Texas. They say that thirteen dollars started the orphanage; today the buildings are worth millions of dollars. The home has housed and clothed thousands of children. Hundreds and hundreds have been saved and sent out to serve God.

When we talk about giving, we think of the story of six-year-old Hattie May Wyatt. The little, dying girl in Philadelphia gave fifty-seven cents to start a new meetinghouse for her church. The pastor, Dr. Russell A. Conwell, took this small sum and, with her dying testimony and example as an inspiration, built the Baptist Temple with an auditorium seating 3,135.

Not only this, Dr. Conwell built Temple University with its enrollment of thousands, the Philadelphia Orphans' Home, three hospitals and a rescue mission.

He delivered one lecture, "Acres of Diamonds," more than six thousand times and with the proceeds helped almost ten thousand young men secure an education.

The little girl's money couldn't buy her life back, but by dying, she gave to Christ. Her investment is still bringing in a measureless harvest to Christ.

•••••

THE WISDOM OF SPURGEON

A wealthy gentleman wrote to the Rev. Charles Haddon Spurgeon urging him to come and preach so they could raise enough funds to pay the debt on the chapel. He offered Spurgeon the use of either his own mansion, his country home or his seaside resort.

Spurgeon promptly replied:

Dear Sir:

Sell one of your places and pay the debt.

Yours very truly,
C. H. Spurgeon

GOD'S WILL

"IN HIS WILL"

In the way of His will, there is peace;
There doubtings and restlessness cease.
Though the pathway be drear, and the sacrifice dear,
In the way of His will, there is peace.

In the place of His will, there is joy;
There praises our hearts will employ.
Amid sorrow and pain, when tears flow like rain,
In the place of His will, there is joy.

In the place of His will, there is power.
His Spirit flows in every hour.
Though our strength may be small,
Though we have none at all,
In the place of His will, there is power.

No life can be at its greatest without submission to God.

• • • •

GOD'S WILL—MOST IMPORTANT!

A few days ago, in the early evening while driving through the streets around our church and Tennessee Temple Schools, I thought of the day when I first arrived in Chattanooga. I thought of the single church building and the pastorium on the adjoining lot. (There was nothing else here.)

As I drove around, I saw the lights in all the buildings of the church and schools. I saw the scores of young people on the sidewalks moving from building to building. I thought of these young people and what they would be doing in years to come. Some will be pastors, some evangelists, many will be missionaries, some teachers in schools, others in the business world.

When I envisioned their future, my heart was blessed. All my disappointments fled. All my heartaches were gone. I prayed, "Lord, let me stay here for a long, long time. This is wonderful."

But He seemed to answer back, "I am glad you like it, but I have something better for you—Heaven!"

His will be done!

Is this your desire? Have you prayed my prayer? Have you been resigned to His answer?

••••

HEAR HIS VOICE AND RESPOND

Thousands of enthusiastic football fans were sitting in the stands waiting for the beginning of the game. As they waited, a little dog strayed from his master onto the field. From one side of the grandstand we heard one whistle. Presently, many were whistling to the dog from all sides.

In the middle of the field the little dog, filled with confusion and fright, crouched to the ground. Then a boy at the end of the field put two fingers in his mouth and whistled shrilly and loudly. The little dog, recognizing his master's call amidst all the others, leaped to his feet. With ears erect, the dog ran swiftly to his master.

I grant you that there may be many confusing calls coming to you in this day. However, if you love the Lord and if you are attentive to His service, you will hear His voice and respond to it.

HEAVEN

OWN ANYTHING UP THERE?

A young minister went to preach in a small country town. There he met a wealthy infidel, a man who had vexed the Christians with his satire and statements of unbelief.

The infidel said to the young preacher, "I want to show you something." He took him to a high elevation on his property and showed him his achievements. "I own everything you see in that direction," he said as he pointed to the north. "I own everything that you see in that direction," and he pointed south, east and west. "I plant on Sunday, harvest on Sunday, yet I have more than all my Christian neighbors put together. How do you explain that?"

The young preacher said, "You have pointed north, south, east and west, and you inform me that you own everything visible in each direction. Let me ask you one question: How much do you own in that direction?" he said, pointing up.

The wealthy unbeliever raised his head to Heaven, then dropped it and said, "I own nothing in that direction."

"What shall it profit a man, if he shall gain the whole world, and lose his own soul?"—Mark 8:36.

••••

IT'S GLORY, YES, IT'S GLORY OVER YONDER!

A dear preacher-friend of mine, Dr. H. H. Savage, who lived in Muskegon, Michigan, was waiting for one of two events: death or the second coming. I believe he didn't really care which one came first. His faith was strong and confident. He knew the Saviour. He was prepared for the future.

For many years Dr. Savage was a successful pastor of the First Baptist Church of Pontiac, Michigan, and for many years, director of the famous Maranatha Bible Conference.

Dr. Savage once conducted a very successful ten-day revival in Highland Park Baptist Church.

Later his body was touched by dreaded cancer, yet his mind was active.

HELL

NO EXITS IN HELL

A few days ago I saw a sermon entitled "Seven Wonders of Hell." The preacher of that sermon said:

The first wonder of Hell is its very existence. When Satan and his hosts rebelled in Heaven and were cast out, then was the "everlasting fire, prepared for the devil and his angels." The skeptics would like to say there is no Hell, but Jesus gave plain teachings on this subject.

The second wonder of Hell is its severe character. The Bible says "everlasting fire." In the story of the rich man and Lazarus, we find the rich man crying out in torment, saying, "For I am tormented in this flame." Hell is a place of gnawing appetite and tormenting desire. Hell is a place of infinite terror of soul.

The third wonder of Hell is that there is no possible way of escape, no exit! When you go into a big auditorium or public hall, you see plainly marked in bold letters EXIT. There is no word *exit* in the vocabulary of Hell. Earth has an exit; for Lazarus and hosts of the saints have gone from earth to Heaven, and a multitude of sinners have gone from earth to Hell. There is an exit from Heaven; for Christ and glorified Moses and Elijah came from Heaven to earth, and Satan and his rebellious demons were cast out of Heaven. There is not an exit from Hell. No one has ever come forth from there. The door of Hell is a trapdoor and swings *in* only.

The fourth wonder of Hell is that this awful condition never ends. Jesus said, "Where their worm dieth not, and the fire is not quenched." The Bible speaks of Hell as a place of everlasting torment. Someone has said, "There are two big Bible words—so big with meaning that we can scarcely comprehend them; and they occur in the Bible but once. The first word is 'eternity' (Isa. 57:15), and the second word is 'Calvary' (Luke 23:33)."

The fifth wonder of Hell is that such a place should be inhabited by all classes of people. Every class, profession, trade, race and age of men and women are found represented among the inhabitants of Hell. There will be those there who were prayed for and were near the point of decision for Christ. There will be those there who have godly mothers or pious wives or husbands. There will be many there who never intended to put off their souls' salvation until it was too late.

The sixth wonder of Hell is that a place of such vile companionships should be so densely inhabited; yet we read, "Wide is the gate, and broad is the way, that leadeth to destruction, and many there be which go in thereat." Think of the multitudes who are stumbling blindly into Hell; but remember, every soul that goes into Hell stumbles over the crucified body of our Lord.

The seventh wonder of Hell is that every inhabitant is praying for mercy rather than cursing the justice of God. In every prison there are those who excuse themselves for the crimes which they have committed and declare that they should be free. In Hell there is no complaint of not having a square deal. It is one continuous cry for mercy which ascends from there. Hear the cry of the rich man, "Father Abraham, have mercy on me."

Men who turn away from Jesus Christ are lost forever, for it is faith that brings salvation.

•   •   •   •

PREACH HEAVEN TO THE SAVED OR HELL TO THE LOST?

On one occasion Duncan Matheson was addressing a

meeting. Over a thousand Christians had gathered to hear the Word of God preached. He read a portion of Scripture that had a wonderful message for Christians and began forthwith to open it up for their edification; but as he thought of poor, needy sinners, he turned to them instead and went on to fill the whole hour with a gospel message.

At the close of the meeting, one of the Christians came up to him and said, "Brother Matheson, it was really too bad. A thousand Christians came here for some spiritual food, and you spent the entire hour preaching the Gospel."

"Oh," said he, "were no unsaved ones there?"

The man answered, "There might have been half a dozen or so."

With a twinkle in his eye, the old man replied in his Scotch accent, "Oh, well, you know Christians—if they are Christians—will manage to wriggle a way to Heaven some way, if they never learn any more truth; but poor sinners have to be saved or go to Hell!"

● ● ● ●

HELL, THE PLACE OF SEPARATION

Separation! What a fearful thing to be separated from our loved ones and peaceful surroundings.

I recall when we heard the news back in Louisville by radio that Floyd Collins was fastened in a cave in Kentucky. He was pinned between rocks in the heart of a cave near Cave City, cut off from light, water, food, warmth and friends.

The nation felt so keenly about rescuing this man that they sent hundreds of men, tons of equipment, and scores of various devices which they thought would rescue him from his lonely prison. Floyd Collins died, separated from all that a man holds dear.

Such is Hell. It is a place of separation. Let us not count this a light matter, for it is a very fearful and awesome fact.

HOLY SPIRIT

"OLD MAN DRYSTICKS" BECAME A LIVE WIRE WHEN FILLED WITH THE SPIRIT

Amazing things happen when the Holy Spirit takes over.

The old Methodist preacher had been called by his parishioners "Old Man Drysticks." Because he was so dry and unattractive, his people were preparing a petition asking for his removal.

The old minister found out what was going on under the surface and, with a broken heart, sought the Saviour's face. All night he cried and prayed, confessing his sins and seeking an enduement of power.

The next Sunday as he preached, the fire fell. His people were amazed. A new grip came into his sermons. A new response came from his pleas. A revival broke out. From night to night souls were saved, and many were added to the church.

The old man who had been called "Old Man Drysticks" became a live wire from Heaven. Now they did not want to get rid of this man but wanted him reappointed to the church.

May God give us the filling of the Holy Spirit!

••••

LET THE HOLY SPIRIT HAVE HIS WAY

Somebody who was critical of D. L. Moody is said to have

asked sneeringly, "Has Dwight L. Moody a monopoly on the Holy Spirit?"

Another person who knew Moody intimately replied, "No, but the Holy Spirit has a monopoly on Dwight L. Moody."

That is exactly what the Holy Spirit wants and what we need. If we let the Holy Spirit have His way, He will work through us the astonishing miracles of God's power; but there must be that submission to the will of Christ.

••••

NO MACHINE BUILT CAN PULL EVIL FROM THE HEART

Dr. R. G. LeTourneau, a great Christian businessman, took us out to show us some of the great machinery he was building—Tournapuls, I think they are called, a word built upon his name.

I dared to ask, "Mr. LeTourneau, have you built the biggest earthmover?"

"Oh no," he replied, "we are just getting started."

He told us about Peru and other parts of the world where they were going to build machines that dwarf any that have been seen up to now. Then looking on that group of men and women, he said, "Friends, the LeTourneau Corporation will never build one big enough to pull one evil habit out of a human heart."

At that, the great Christian businessman pointed his finger upward in token of his acceptance of the fact that only the power of the new birth can take evil out of our lives.

••••

THE HOLY SPIRIT COMES UPON THOSE WHO WALK IN HIS WAY

Dr. M. E. Dodd, pastor for many years of the First Baptist Church in Shreveport, Louisiana, used to tell the story of going through the Bible on his knees. He would open his Bible, place it on a chair; then on his knees by that chair, he would read a chapter. He bears witness that it was one of the richest experiences that he had ever had.

One snowy morning he entered his study as usual, opened the Bible at the third chapter of Ephesians—one of the richest passages in all the Bible—but everything was as cold on the inside as it was on the outside. There was no moving of the Spirit.

He stopped trying to read, placed his face in his hands and prayed, "O Lord, if You will show me what is wrong, I'll right it, no matter what the cost."

Immediately there flashed through his mind that the night before his wife had told him of a widow with three children who had no fuel. He arose, put on his overshoes and overcoat, and went to the alley where the woman lived.

He knocked on the door, and a timid voice said, "Come in." He entered and found a woman in bed with her children. Not a spark of fire was in the grate nor a crust of bread in the cupboard.

Dr. Dodd called the coal man to bring some coal and called the women of the church to bring some food. He hunted up some kindling and had it in the grate by the time the coal man arrived. He placed the coal on the kindling and lit the fire. The good women began to come in with steaming hot food.

Dr. Dodd went back to his room, got down on his knees by the same chair, and opened his Bible at the same chapter. He said the very heavens fell with power.

The Holy Spirit comes upon those who walk in His way. When we follow after Jesus, we will be considerate of others, and there will be a definite purpose in living.

● ● ● ●

A THOUSAND MISTAKES
WITHOUT HIS POWER

Dr. C. Oscar Johnson, for many years pastor of the Third Baptist Church in St. Louis, used to illustrate a great truth with this story from his boyhood:

> My father was a blacksmith, and I spent much time pumping the bellows that made the fire hot. He never bought ready-made horseshoes. He made them. He would put a strip of iron in the fire and leave it until it was white-hot, then holding it with a pair of tongs, bend it around the anvil by tapping it lightly with a hammer. When it was the right size and shape for the horse he was shoeing, he would heat it again and turn the ends down to make the cleats.
>
> It seemed so easy that one day when we were not busy, I asked him to let me make one. A smile of amusement broke over his face as he answered, "All right. I'll pump the bellows, and you make the shoe."
>
> When the strip of iron was hot, I took it off the forge and tried to bend it around the circular end of the anvil. The more I hammered, the funnier it looked. It was twisted and lopsided. I was deeply chagrined.
>
> My father took the tongs and held up the shoe. He shook his head and said, "Son, I never saw the horse that could wear that shoe," and tossed it back into the fire. After a moment he said, "Let's make one together."

I have made a thousand mistakes when I did something by myself, but never a single one when I depended upon the Heavenly Father and the Holy Spirit's power.

•••

"YOU CAN'T PAINT LIKE THE GREAT
MASTER UNLESS YOU HAVE
HIS SPIRIT"

A young Italian boy knocked on the door of an artist's studio in Rome. When it was opened, he said, "Please, Madam, would you give me the master's brush?" The painter had died, and the young boy, inflamed with the longing to be an artist, wished for the great master's brush.

The lady placed the brush in the youth's hand, saying, "This is his brush. Try it, my boy."

With a flush of earnestness on his face, he made a supreme effort but soon found that he could paint no better with it than with his own.

The lady then said, "Remember, my child, you cannot paint like the great master unless you have his spirit."

Many of us would like to be like the Apostle Paul, but we must remember that Paul was controlled by the Spirit of God. He turned away from the self-life and lived completely under God's divine direction.

• • • •

"ARE YOU FILLED WITH THE HOLY SPIRIT NOW?"

Question yourself on this important matter: does Christ have the place in your life that He should have?

I remember so vividly a message I gave at Rumney, New Hampshire, some years ago. As I recall the experience, I spoke in sincerity on the fullness of the Holy Spirit.

I finished my message and started back to the cabin where I was staying. As I crossed the grounds, a young man, about twenty-five years of age, stopped me and said, "Sir, I heard your message a few moments ago. It blessed me and helped me. I do not want you to think that I am a smart aleck or that I am trying to pry into your affairs, but I would like to know: are you filled with the Holy Spirit now?"

I felt no anger because of such a question; rather, I felt humbled because it caused me to examine my own heart. Could it be that I had been speaking on the fullness of the Holy Spirit and failed to possess at that moment the fullness of the truth which I had been expounding?

O Christian friend, let the Holy Spirit take over in your life. Let Him fully possess and use you. Let your life be under His direct control.

JESUS CHRIST

HIS BLOOD CAN MAKE THEE
WHITER THAN THE SNOW

The author of this poem is unknown, but the message is good for us all.

When Jesus came to Golgotha,
  They hanged Him on a tree;
They drove great nails through hands and feet
  And made a Calvary.

They crowned Him with a crown of thorns;
  Red were His wounds and deep;
For those were crude and cruel days,
  And human flesh was cheap.

When Jesus came to our town,
  They simply passed Him by;
They did not hurt a hair of Him;
  They only watched Him die;

For men had grown more tender—
  They would not cast a stone;
They only passed Him on the street
  And left Him there alone.

Still Jesus cried, "Forgive them,
  For they know not what they do";
He prays that prayer for us tonight,
  For you, and you, and you.

We pass Him by and leave Him there,
  Without an eye to see;
And crucify our Lord afresh,
  As He prays on Calvary.

O sinner, listen to this last appeal:

It matters not how dark thy sin may be:
The blood of Jesus still avails for thee;
Though heavy be thy load of guilt and woe,
His blood can make thee whiter than the snow.

••••

LORD, SHOW ME MYSELF; LORD, SHOW ME THYSELF

Dr. R. A. Torrey told a very strange and interesting story of a faithful Scottish minister who was traveling through Scotland and stopped one night at an inn. The innkeeper came to him and asked if he would conduct family worship. He replied that he would if the innkeeper would bring to the family worship all the guests in the house and also the servants. This the innkeeper agreed to do.

When they were gathered in the big room for the service, the minister turned to the innkeeper and said, "Are all the servants here?"

"Yes," replied the innkeeper.

"All?" insisted the minister.

"Well, all but one. One girl who works down in the kitchen washing the pots and kettles is so dirty that she is not fit to come to the meeting."

The minister replied, "We will not go on with the service until she comes."

The innkeeper went for this servant and brought her in. This faithful man of God became greatly interested in this poor, neglected creature. When the others were passing out of the room, he asked her to stay for a few minutes. When everyone had gone, he said to her, "I want to teach you a prayer for you to make: 'Lord, show me myself.' Will you pray it every day?" She replied that she would.

The next day the minister left, but in a few days he came

back and asked the innkeeper about this girl. The innkeeper replied, "She is spoiled. She weeps all the time, day and night, weeps so that she can hardly attend to her work."

The minister asked to see her again. When she came in, he said, "Now I want to teach you another prayer: 'Lord, show me Thyself.' Now pray that prayer every day."

The Scotch minister left.

A few years afterward he was preaching one Lord's Day in a church in Glasgow. At the close of the service, a neat, trim-looking young woman came up to him and said, "Do you recognize me?"

"No, I do not."

"Do you recall holding a service in an inn and speaking to one of the servants afterward and teaching her to pray the prayer, 'Lord, show me myself,' then teaching her the other prayer, 'Lord, show me Thyself'?"

"Oh yes, I remember that."

"Well, I am that girl, and when you taught me that first prayer and went away, I asked God to show me myself. He gave me such a view of my vileness and my sin that I was overwhelmed with grief and could scarcely sleep at night or work by day for thinking of my sins. Then, when you came back and taught me the second prayer, 'Lord, show me Thyself,' God gave me such a view of Himself, of His love, of Jesus Christ dying on the cross for me, that all the burden of my sin rolled away, and I became a happy Christian."

Sinner friend, will you pray these two prayers: "Lord, show me myself," and, "Lord, show me Thyself"? Christians, will you do the same? Will you ask the Holy Spirit to reveal to you your needs and impress upon you the worthwhileness of simple trust in Him and complete dedication of your all to His will?

• • • •

PUT CHRIST FIRST, THEN
SEE HIM WORK

In your life and mine, Christ must have the preeminence. When we put Him in the right place, there is a purpose for living.

Down in Mississippi someone told me this story about Mr. R. G. LeTourneau, known as the "earth-moving man," with all his heavy equipment.

It was a Wednesday, and Mr. LeTourneau wanted to go to prayer meeting, yet he had promised some men to have a certain device ready for them on the next day. It would take many hours to develop the mechanism.

After pondering it over for awhile, he came to a decision to let Christ have first place.

He went to prayer meeting, received a blessing, and when the service was over, he returned to his workshop. As he sat down, the full solution to his problem was given him; and in less than ten minutes he had finished the design for a piece of machinery which had puzzled his men for many days.

Put Christ first and see Him work out your problems.

• • • •

THE MASTER MAKES THE DIFFERENCE

I read of a little girl who used to annoy guests at a hotel by her piano practice every afternoon. It was monotonous for the little girl but maddening for the guests, since she had to practice on a public piano.

One day when a distinguished guest heard the others complaining of her annoyance, he walked over and sat down beside her.

As she practiced her simple exercises, he, a great musician himself, took those exercises and began to weave around and through them great and sublime harmonies. As he and the little girl played, the guests began drifting into the room, entranced by the beautiful music.

So it is that the Master of men will come into our lives and will take our efforts and weave in and through them His high and holy purposes, and the world will hear the great message of divine love through our humble efforts.

••••

GOD CAN TRANSFORM SOMETHING USE-LESS INTO SOMETHING BEAUTIFUL

A handful of sand is deposited by the Lord in the heart of the earth. Great heat is applied from beneath and ponderous weight from above. When found by man it has become a beautiful, fiery opal.

God does the same thing with clay, and man finds a lovely amethyst. He does the same thing with black carbon, and man finds a glorious diamond. How? I don't know. I only know that He can take a useless and fruitless life and transform it into a beautiful garden of the sweetest graces for His glory.

What is this illustration saying to us? Simply this: Christ can take a poor lost sinner and save him and transform him into a beautiful saint.

"For when we were yet without strength, in due time Christ died for the ungodly.

"For scarcely for a righteous man will one die: yet peradventure for a good man some would even dare to die.

"But God commendeth his love toward us, in that, while we were yet sinners, Christ died for us."—Rom. 5:6–8.

••••

CHRIST AT EVERY TABLE, IN EVERY CONVERSATION

At the close of World War I, an artist drew a cartoon of a group of men around a conference table hoping to organize the new world—the president, secretary of war, secretary of state and some others. Then the cartoon showed a new, strange figure at the council table—Christ, as the secretary of human relations.

The cartoon of the artist must become a reality: Christ at every table; Christ in every conversation; Christ in every deal; Christ primary in every election.

• • • •

A LIFE IN THE MASTER'S HANDS CAN LIFT MAN TOWARD GOD

Many years ago a famous violinist gave a concert in a western town. When it was over, a gray-haired pastor was seen talking to the violinist. The next day the town was flooded with handbills saying:

> Come to the First Baptist Church tonight and hear the famous violinist play on his five-thousand-dollar violin. No admission charge.

That night the church was crowded. The violinist came out and played his first number. The people had never heard such beautiful music. They laughed and they cried. They applauded at the end of the number.

The violinist smiled and began to tighten his violin strings. Suddenly one of them snapped. In a fit of anger, the man lifted the violin above his head and brought it down on the pulpit, shattering it to pieces. He then sat down.

The crowd was astounded that this man would destroy a five-thousand-dollar violin; but the pastor came to the pulpit and said, "The violin which the artist used to stir your souls was worth sixty-four cents. The five-thousand-dollar one is behind the curtain, and he will play it for you in a moment. Learn a lesson: A sixty-four-cent violin in the master's hand can make music fit for God's symphony orchestra.

A little life in the hands of Jesus, the Master, can lift man toward God."

Limited vessels? Yes, we are; but as we give ourselves to the Lord, He will make us vessels meet for the Master's use.

• • • •

TO BE LIKE CHRIST, WALK IN HIS STEPS

In the last World War a certain soldier's face was horribly disfigured. When he realized his condition, he lost all interest in life and wished to die. A surgeon came and told him that he could operate on his face and perhaps restore it, if he had some picture to go by.

The soldier didn't have a picture, so he said, "It's no use, Doctor. Just leave me alone."

"But," said the doctor, "I can do something for you. Just pick out any picture, and I will make your face like that picture."

"Oh, it doesn't matter," insisted the soldier; "but that picture on the wall will be all right." (The soldier didn't know it, but it was a picture of Christ.)

The doctor performed the operation, and it was highly successful. The soldier was greatly pleased when he looked in the mirror after he had fully recovered.

"Whose picture was that?" he asked the doctor.

The doctor told him it was a picture of Jesus.

"What kind of a man was He?" he asked.

The doctor gave him a New Testament and told him to read about Jesus.

When the doctor came back to see him in a few days, the soldier said, "There is just one thing for me to do. Since I look like Him, I have resolved that I must be like Him. I will here and now receive Him as my Saviour, and I want to walk in His steps."

"For even hereunto were ye called: because Christ also suffered

for us, leaving us an example, that ye should follow his steps."—
I Pet. 2:21.

• • • •

"I KNOW THE AUTHOR"

A large dinner party was taking place in New York City.
A very wealthy lady was seated by the side of a learned professor of science.

In the course of the conversation, she said quite naturally,
"The Bible says so and so."

"The Bible!" remarked the professor. "You don't believe
the Bible?"

"Yes, indeed, I believe it," replied the lady.

"Why, I didn't suppose any intelligent person today
believed the Bible!"

"Oh, yes," she said. "I believe it all. I know the Author."

• • • •

"THE KING IS STILL WITH YOU"

An interesting story is told of Victor Immanuel III
of Italy.

The leader of his country was fighting along with his soldiers against their enemy. In the midst of the battle, a lieutenant was wounded. The wounded officer called for a soldier and gave him a few keepsakes and bade him to take
them to his family. He ordered him to fly from the battle-
field, but the soldier tried to carry the lieutenant to a place
of safety. Some gunners urged him to save himself, but still
he remained, struggling to protect his load.

A motor horn sounded, and the whisper went around that
the king had left the field, but the soldier struggled on.
Finally the lieutenant died in his arms.

Throwing himself on the corpse of his dead officer,

the young soldier exclaimed tearfully, "Even the king has gone away!"

Just then a hand was laid upon his shoulder. Looking up, he found himself looking into the face of the king. Saluting, he stood at attention.

"My boy, the car has gone, but the king is still with you."

Yes, Christ is the Good Shepherd, and He is still with us. He suffered, bled and died; He rose again and ascended into Heaven; and as the Good Shepherd is watching over us, He places Himself between us and our dangers.

••••

THE WAY OUT IS CHRIST

An artist said to a class of art students, "When you paint a picture of the woods or forest, always paint a path leading out. If you don't have this path, those who look at the picture will have the feeling of suffocation."

The picture of the conditions of this day is not pleasant, but, thank God, the way out is Jesus Christ who said, "I am the way." He leads the way to safety, to satisfaction and to salvation. He is the way to our hope, our happiness, and to our home in Heaven.

••••

BEWARE OF ANYTHING THAT TRIES TO HIDE EVIL

I had placed in my hands a newspaper from Memphis, Tennessee. It gave a big writeup on what was taking place in the city of Memphis. It told about the churches that are leading in experimenting with new things to interest young people. The staff writer of the Memphis paper said about the new music of the present day: "There is plenty of movement in this show, including handclapping, modern dance movements, rock music, psychedelic lighting and effects in the background."

He went on to say: "Beautiful young voices sing powerful new songs which comment on such things as the friction between generations, ecological problems, and churches which put programs ahead of people."

The writer added, "They use electric guitars, electric organ, piano, trumpets, trombones and frenetic drumbeats to register their protest against the programmed church."

The writer also said that thirty or forty churches in Memphis, Tennessee, are now using "folk musicals." The director of one of these musicals said, "Young people want rock music but not the 'Rock of Ages.' The new young Christians sometimes feel out of place in today's church, but it's what's happening, Baby."

My comment is this: Beware of the movement today that tries to hide evil, fleshly acts under the name of Christ. We are failing to present the Saviour as the Bible presents Him.

••••

ALL AUTHORITY IN JESUS

Someone said this: "Jesus had no earthly possessions. At His birth He was laid in a borrowed manger; He preached a sermon from a borrowed boat; He rode into Jerusalem on a borrowed beast; He ate His last supper with His apostles in a borrowed room; He was buried in a borrowed grave. Yet the living, risen Son of God said, 'All power [authority] is given unto me in heaven and in earth.'"

It matters not who you may be. In your heart there is a place for the Son of God. Let Him be the King of Kings and the Lord of Lords of your life.

••••

KEEP YOUR EYES FIXED ON JESUS, AND YOU WILL GROW IN HIS LIKENESS

Many of you have heard the legend of the prince whose back was bowed and bent—a hunchback. Because of this physical deformity, he was quite sensitive.

One day he sent for the best sculptor in the province and asked him to make a statue of his likeness but with the back straight: "I want to see myself as I might have been."

The sculptor did as he was commissioned, then brought the finished work to the prince. It was well done, a striking likeness with a straight back.

The prince had the statue placed in a secret nook in the royal garden. Every day he would secretly steal to the spot and look at himself as he would have been with a straight back. Each time he saw it, something seemed to happen on the inside of him. After awhile the people began to notice that the prince was not as bent as he once was.

Then one day while he was in the garden standing up close to the statue, he saw that he was as straight as it was!

The application is a simple one: If we will keep our eyes fixed upon the Lord Jesus, we will grow in His likeness.

We used to sing on our "Back Home Hour" broadcasts:

Turn your eyes upon Jesus,
Look full in His wonderful face;
And the things of earth will grow strangely dim
In the light of His glory and grace.

• • • •

WE FIND NOT ONE FAULT WITH JESUS

In a magazine coming to my desk, I read an article written by a U.S. Presbyterian elder and deacon entitled "There Are Some Things About Jesus I Don't Like." This

Presbyterian then pointed out many things about Jesus he didn't like.

He said, "The idea that Jesus even believed in such things as Hell and the Devil is rather degrading to a religion trying to exist in this enlightened age." He also said, "A sensible person realizes that a God of love could not allow such a thing as Hell to exist as reality. It seems more acceptable to me to think of Hell as being separated from God, and the Devil, merely as the absence of good."

Then he went on to say that he does not like Christ's attitude toward race relations, and he criticized the deeds of Christ and the healing power of our Saviour.

This man may write an article entitled "There Are Some Things About Christ I Don't Like," but I find not one single thing in this Bible that I do not like. I believe in Christ Jesus the Lord, the Saviour of mankind, the eternal, infallible Son of God. I know myself as a poor, weak, finite individual, but I look to the Lord as that eternal Holy One who came to this world to die for sinners such as you and me and who is our Saviour through our faith in Him.

••••

"I FOUND CHRIST SUFFICIENT"

There is an interesting story about Commander Booth Tucker of the Salvation Army. This man had been an officer in the Indian Army, but he resigned when he fell under the spell of Jesus and joined the Salvation Army.

In time this Englishman met and married the daughter of General Booth, founder of the Salvation Army. They were sent to America, and he became a great leader in the Midwest.

One night as he was preaching in Chicago, he said that Jesus Christ was equal to any demand that can come to a man.

A man far back in the audience rose to his feet and said,

"Booth Tucker, I challenge your statement. If you were as I am, with five children who have been robbed of their mother through death, and hearing them cry for one who cannot come, would you say that Christ is sufficient?"

Booth Tucker closed the meeting and tried to reason with this man, but to no avail.

Five or six days later, there was a train crash in Chicago, and Booth Tucker's own wife was killed. Two days afterward he was again in the great auditorium where he had spoken the week before. Standing beside the body of his dead wife, Booth Tucker said simply, "I do not know whether my friend of seven days ago is here or not, but I wish to say that I now stand where he stands. My children also cry for one who cannot come; but I want to tell him that in these two days of darkness, *I have found Christ sufficient."*

••••

LOOK FOR THE NAILPRINTS

A religious fanatic was speaking to a group on a street corner. He wore a long white robe and had a long beard. He declared that he was Christ come back upon the earth.

A Christian man walked up to him and said, "Let me see your hands." When the man held out his hands, the Christian said, "You are not my Christ. There are no nailprints."

No one can deceive us. Christ is coming for us, and we shall see Him, and we shall know Him; indeed, we know Him even now.

••••

THE ACCESSIBLE SAVIOUR

I got a thrill the other day reading the story of a man named Bill Walford.

Many years ago Bill lived in Coleshill, England. He whittled novelties for children, and he made a scant living by carving items out of ivory and selling them in a little shop. He had many difficulties, but his faith in God led him through every trial.

Though only a layman, Walford was often asked to preach in churches. There was something uplifting about this man's outlook on life.

One day in 1842, a minister, Thomas Salmon, stopped in Walford's shop and found his friend occupied with more than his artistic carvings. Walford had a poem on prayer running through his mind, so he asked Brother Salmon to take down the words as he recited them while they were still fresh in his memory. Walford had a rare spiritual insight, but he asked for help because he was physically blind.

His friend wrote down the words. Years later they came to the attention of an organist William Bradbury. He saw the poem and put it to music. Do you know its name? "Sweet Hour of Prayer." Bill Walford, a blind whittler of Coleshill, England, was the author of that lovely song.

> Sweet hour of prayer! sweet hour of prayer!
> That calls me from a world of care,
> And bids me at my Father's throne
> Make all my wants and wishes known;
> In seasons of distress and grief,
> My soul has often found relief,
> And oft escaped the tempter's snare
> By thy return, sweet hour of prayer.
>
> Sweet hour of prayer! sweet hour of prayer!
> The joys I feel, the bliss I share
> Of those whose anxious spirits burn
> With strong desires for thy return!
> With such I hasten to the place
> Where God my Saviour shows His face,
> And gladly take my station there,
> And wait for thee, sweet hour of prayer.
>
> Sweet hour of prayer! sweet hour of prayer!

> Thy wings shall my petition bear
> To Him whose truth and faithfulness
> Engage the waiting soul to bless;
> And since He bids me seek His face,
> Believe His Word and trust His grace,
> I'll cast on Him my every care,
> And wait for thee, sweet hour of prayer.

Bill Walford knew that Christ was accessible. He came to Him with his needs, and he gave to the world one of the sweetest songs on prayer we have ever had.

••••

"I CAN NEVER USE MY BRUSH TO PAINT AN INFERIOR SUBJECT!"

When the renowned artist Dannecker was requested by Napoleon to make a painting of Venus, he declined, even though an enormous sum was offered. The emperor's anger was stirred, and he demanded an explanation. The painter answered simply, "I have painted Christ, and I can never use my brush to paint an inferior subject."

The story is that when he finished his first painting of the Saviour, he uncovered the canvas on which he had toiled many years. His little daughter admired it with delight. When asked who she thought it was, she replied that it surely must be some great man. In bitter disappointment, Dannecker destroyed his painting and started over again.

Other years passed; and when the painting was again completed, the result of much toil and prayer, the daughter was brought before the new painting. She was asked who she thought it was. The girl went reverently to the painting and said, "This is the One who said, 'Suffer little children to come unto me.'"

Dannecker felt that he would have failed had his child not recognized the subject of his painting as the divine Son of God.

••••

"EVERYONE STAND WHILE OUR BROTHER LEADS THE AUDIENCE IN WEEPING"

Years ago in Los Angeles a well-known preacher had the art of making his people laugh and enjoy themselves during a sermon. He would tell funny stories, then use expressions to bring laughter.

However, one day in the service a critic, out of harmony with the entire occasion, stood and with open rebuke said, "I do not think this is either the place or the time to laugh. We should be weeping instead of laughing."

After a proper amount of silence, the preacher said, "I shall ask everyone to stand while our brother leads the audience in weeping."

The world is filled with too many sad things. Tears are in every home, along every highway, in the workplace—nowhere are we free of tears, but in Christ there is rejoicing!

• • • •

"I AM THE WAY"

A missionary engaged a guide to take him across a desert country. When the two men arrived at the edge of the desert, the missionary, looking ahead, saw trackless sand without a single footprint or road.

Turning to his guide, he asked in a tone of surprise, "Where is the road?"

With a reproving glance, the guide replied, "*I* am the road."

Let's turn that simple story around and let Christ be the One who says, "I am the way, the truth, and the life: no man cometh unto the Father, but by me."

• • • •

"I HAVE THE BEST PILOT THERE IS—CHRIST"

Dr. F. C. McConnell, one time pastor of the First Baptist

Church of Anderson, South Carolina, told about a plane trip that he took in Europe. The air became rough. The passengers began to get sick. The storm raged more furiously. At every gust of wind, the plane was whipped and tossed like a toy.

Some of the passengers were frightened. Death seemed inevitable. A little black-headed Norwegian stewardess did her best to cheer the discouraged people. She adjusted safety belts, rearranged pillows, and comforted the sick.

Suddenly she started speaking over and over again a quick phrase that seemed to work miracles: "Remember, the best pilot in Europe is in charge of this plane."

Dr. McConnell said, "It is that way in life. When the storm gets rough, and I wonder if I am going to get through, I remember that while the storm rages, I have the best Pilot there is—Christ."

LIVING

"BE CAREFUL FOR NOTHING"

"Be careful for nothing; but in every thing by prayer and supplication with thanksgiving let your requests be made known unto God.

"And the peace of God, which passeth all understanding, shall keep your hearts and minds through Christ Jesus."—Phil. 4:6,7.

It was J. Hudson Taylor, the great missionary to China, who made this comment upon these verses:

> Do we fail to be anxious for nothing and to bring everything by prayer and supplication, with thanksgiving, before God? We may bring nine difficulties out of ten to Him and try to manage the tenth ourselves; and that one little difficulty, like a small leak that runs the vessel dry, is fatal to the whole. Like a small breach in a city wall, it gives entrance to the power of the foe; but if we fulfill the conditions, He is certainly faithful, and instead of our having to keep our hearts and minds—our affections and thoughts—we shall find them kept for us.
>
> The peace which we can neither make nor keep, will itself, as a garrison, keep and protect us; and the cares and worries which strive to enter, will do so in vain.

••••

"PUT AWAY ALL BITTERNESS"

While Dr. R. W. Hubert was holding a revival meeting in a fine country church, he stayed in the home of the chairman of the board of deacons.

He preached Sunday, Monday, Tuesday and Wednesday, but nothing happened. Then on Thursday morning as he sat on the front porch ready for the morning service, the deacon's daughter came out and said, "Brother Hubert, we are having a great meeting."

"Why do you say that?" he asked.

"Because of what it has done for my father," was her reply.

He said, "Tell me about it."

The young woman said: "I have a younger sister named Emily. A year ago she graduated from high school, and Father wanted her to go to college. She was in love with a grocery clerk in a town twenty miles away. They wanted to get married, but Father put his foot down and said, 'You are not going to marry anyone. You are going to college first.'

"But you know how young people are when they are in love. One afternoon, Emily and John went over to the county seat and got married. When they came back home, Father was furious. 'Emily, take your clothes and leave. I don't ever want to see you again.'

"For the past year, Emily has not been allowed to come home, and Mother and I never get to see her. She and John live in a town twenty miles away. However, something has happened to Father. Last Sunday when you preached your first sermon, he asked the pastor if he had told the visiting preacher anything about him. When the pastor said he had not, Father said, 'But he hit me right between the eyes this morning.'

"Just after breakfast this morning, Father said to Mother, 'Call Emily and tell her and John to come over and spend the day with us on Sunday and eat dinner with us and go to our meeting.'

"Mother said, 'Dad, you were the one who drove her away, and you will have to be the one who invites her back.'

"So Father called. 'Emily, this is your father. We are having a good meeting at the church. We want you and John to come and spend the day with us, eat dinner with us, and go to church.' Emily said they would come."

Dr. Hubert said that on Sunday, the church was filled when the service began. The deacons sat in the "Amen Corner." The father was watching the door to see John and Emily when they came in.

Finally they came and started down the aisle. The deacon forgot all of his dignity, ran up the aisle, and met them. He threw one big arm around Emily and one big arm around John; and there before the whole congregation they wept and laughed and made up their differences.

Dr. Hubert said he didn't preach that morning. He just gave an invitation, and thirty-five people came forward to give their hearts to Christ. One was the deacon's son who had stayed out of church because of his father's bitter attitude.

Yes, our lives need to conform to the Bible. If they do not, then trouble is bound to overtake us, and this hinders others.

You see what it did to one family. Then you see what happened when bitterness was put away. It not only fixed a family, but it brought revival.

• • • •

PADEREWSKI'S PUPIL

Paderewski arrived in a small Connecticut town about noon one day and decided to take a walk in the afternoon. While strolling along he heard a piano and, following the sound, came to a house on which was a sign reading:

| MISS JONES. PIANO LESSONS. |
| 25 CENTS AN HOUR. |

Pausing to listen, he heard the young woman trying to play one of Chopin's nocturnes and not succeeding very well.

Paderewski walked up to the house and knocked.

Miss Jones came to the door and recognized him at once. Delighted, she invited him in; and he sat down and played the nocturne as only he could, afterward spending an hour correcting her mistakes. Miss Jones thanked him, and he departed.

Some months later he returned to the town, and again he took the same walk.

He soon came to the home of Miss Jones; and looking at the sign, he read:

> MISS JONES (PUPIL OF PADEREWSKI):
> PIANO LESSONS $1.00 AN HOUR.

••••

NEEDED: DAILY CHECKUP

I think it was F. B. Meyer who said that we should "keep close accounts with God."

What the great Bible teacher was simply saying was that every day we should have a daily checkup on our lives to see how it is between us and our Lord—that there are no hidden, unclean corners, nothing swept under the rug. We are to pray and confess any sin, then seek His will in honesty and in submissiveness.

••••

HUMILITY TRIUMPHED

Dr. Samuel Logan Brengle was a brilliant American university student, the leading orator of his day. Upon graduation he was called to the pulpit of an influential church where he was acclaimed a coming pulpiteer, but his heart was not satisfied. He did not feel that he was reaching enough people and longed to do more to spread the Gospel.

At this crucial time he read of the Salvation Army, then regarded as a rather disreputable organization. As he read of its achievements among the underprivileged of Britain and the trophies it was winning from the gutter, he felt this was the type work that would satisfy his heart's yearning. He resigned his church, sailed for London, and offered his services to General William Booth. He was ultimately accepted for service; but in order to test his caliber, he was put in the training garrison with scores of cadets, most of whom, though full of zeal, were innocent of formal education.

His first work was to clean a pile of muddy boots belonging to his fellow students. As he brushed away the mud, a battle royal raged in his heart. Was it for this he had renounced his fashionable church and come to London? The Devil pressed the advantages that he had gained, and Brengle had almost succumbed to the tempter's voice when a verse of Scripture was injected into his mind by the Holy Spirit: "He...took a towel, and girded himself." In a moment he detected the subtlety of his adversary, and from his heart he cried, "Lord, if Thou couldest take a towel and wash the disciples' dirty feet, surely I can take a brush and clean the cadets' dirty boots."

Humility triumphed, and the victory laid the foundation for a life which multiplied itself a thousandfold in a worldwide ministry.

••••

"YOU PAID FOR THOSE MEALS WHEN YOU BOUGHT YOUR TICKET"

Dr. Herschel Ford tells about a certain man who was traveling on a great ocean liner going from London to New York. Day after day he ate cheese and crackers. At lunchtime on the last day out, one of the ship's officers found him sitting in one of the deck chairs eating his lunch of cheese and crackers.

The officer asked him, "Why don't you go into the ship's dining room and eat with the other passengers?"

The man replied, "I can't afford it."

"My man," said the officer, "you paid for those meals when you bought your ticket. It would have cost you nothing to have eaten all your meals on this ship."

There are some Christians like that: they take salvation from the hands of the Lord, then refuse to come to Him with every burden and care.

Come, walk with our Saviour as you travel the road of sorrow. Take what He offers with thanksgiving.

••••

LET YOUR LIGHT SHINE!

A few years ago William Jennings Bryan said, "An atheist can find an answer for every argument you can offer, except the argument of a consistent Christian life."

How true! It is the presence of Christ lighting a man's life that gives that life attractiveness and beauty. That light transforms ordinary men and women into saints and sometimes martyrs for our Lord. When Stephen was stoned to death, his face was made to *shine* like an angel's.

One of the weaknesses of our day is we are so afraid to let others know that we are Christians. We try to hide our religion with the cares of the world so no one can discover that we believe in Christ and follow Him! God help us.

May Christ touch and change every life. May we be shining lights for others to see. It matters not whether you are a day laborer or a company executive, whether you belong to the poor class or to the rich class. There should be a glorious testimony to the world that we are not following the world but Christ.

"Let your light so shine before men, that they may see your good works, and glorify your Father which is in heaven."—Matt. 5:16.

••••

TOYING WITH TRIFLES

Many a Christian has had great problems because of trying to get ahead of someone else. Reaching for riches and reaching for fame have been common stumbling blocks. It is so easy to waste a life on minor matters.

I recall the home of a fine man who was pastor of a large church. The wife rarely took any part in church affairs, wanting to spend all her time at home. This was her god, and she said so! Everything had to be just perfect—every table, every chair, every book had an exact spot. She became terribly troubled if anything was moved. She was "toying with trifles."

I think you can imagine the conclusion of that story.

It is good for us to know what is small and what is large. Magnify the things that are important and minimize the small things of life.

• • • •

A WEALTHY PAUPER

In a book sent to me some time ago, I read the true story of "a wealthy pauper."

A frail little widow was found starving to death in her dreary New York City flat. Four days later, at age ninety, she died of starvation. The widow, known as "Miss Emma" by her Staten Island neighbors, left a fortune of about half a million dollars. There was $275,000 in currency carelessly crammed into cardboard boxes and hoarded in her closet. In addition to the money in the apartment, Miss Emma had more than $200,000 in banks. She also owned hundreds of shares of stock.

Miss Emma's six-room flat above a store was dusty, and its windows, curtainless. Her sizable wealth had apparently gone untouched while she lived on fifteen-cent hot dogs. She gathered up boxes and wrappings for her old pot-bellied stove so she could save on gas and electric bills.

Possessor of great wealth, Miss Emma lived and died as a pauper.

This is a little picture of the selfishness of our day. People seek to gain for themselves and refuse to give to a lost and dying world. This is a picture of many of our churches—wealthy in properties and buildings but poverty-stricken in soul. This is the picture of many Christians who are selfishly holding everything to themselves and refusing to give a thing to the work of God.

• • • •

"I'M ON THE WRONG BOAT!"

Dr. A. C. Dixon told about two steamers tied up side by side in one of the lakes in the North. One boat had been engaged by a Christian organization. The other was used to take men to a certain spot where they raced their horses and engaged in betting and drinking.

The boat for Christians left every hour for a camp meeting on the other side of the lake. The boat going to the place of festivity, gaiety and dissipation also left the same hour.

A man came running down to the water's edge as one boat was leaving for the camp meeting. By mistake, he jumped in. The boat was soon out some distance from shore when the people started singing:

Rock of Ages, cleft for me,
Let me hide myself in Thee.

The man's face paled with the pallor of death. Then when the song was finished, someone said, "Let us have a moment of prayer," and someone led in a fervent prayer.

When the prayer was finished, a young man stood up and said, "May I tell you of the great experience I had last week in answer to prayer? It was a marvelous evidence to me that God is alive and very near and takes cognizance of the cry of His people." Then he told the story, and they sang another hymn.

By this time, the poor latecomer to the boat found the captain and said to him, "Let me off! This is intolerable. This is Hell to me. Let me off! I'm on the wrong boat. I'm in the wrong company. I am out of place."

Yes, salvation ought to mean a change of direction, going another way, singing different songs, living a different lifestyle.

•••

"IF YOU ARE ACCUSED OF BEING A CHRISTIAN, IS THERE ENOUGH PROOF TO CONVICT YOU?"

A visitor went to a home and knocked on the door. A man answered the knock. The visitor introduced himself, then said, "I was wondering, sir, if you have membership in any church."

The man of the house said quickly, "Oh yes, I do belong to a church and have belonged for many years. I joined the church before I was married."

The wife, sitting in the room, spoke up, "Imagine that! We have been married twenty years, and this is the first time I knew that he belonged to a church."

You have heard it said, "If you are accused of being a Christian, is there enough proof to convict you?"

Do you bear the characteristics and marks of a Christian?

•••

ONLY USEFUL WHEN APPLIED

My friend, the Gospel works when it is received.

A non-Christian soap manufacturer was walking with a minister. Said the soapmaker, "The Gospel you preach hasn't done much good, for there are still a lot of wickedness and wicked people."

The preacher made no immediate reply. Soon they passed an exceedingly dirty child making mud pies, and the preacher said, "Soap hasn't done much good in the world, I see; for there are still much dirt and many dirty people."

"Oh well," answered the manufacturer, "soap is only useful when it is applied."

"Exactly," was the minister's reply, "and so it is with the Gospel."

••••

NO SITE AS BEAUTIFUL AS SOULS

Old Uncle Bud Robinson was a Holiness preacher.

Many years ago some friends took him with them to New York. They showed him the skyscrapers, the ships going out and coming in from Europe, the subway, and other interesting sites.

That evening Uncle Bud prayed, "Lord, I thank You that I got to see this big city today—the skyscrapers, the ships going out and coming in, and so many other places; but, Lord, the thing for which I want to thank You most of all is, I didn't see a thing I wanted."

Watch yourself when you are more concerned about money than you are about the souls of men. Watch yourself when you are more concerned about salaries than getting sinners saved. We must be concerned. We must be burdened for the lost.

••••

DO WE LIVE TO PLEASE THE FATHER?

Dr. William Hatcher was a greatly used man of God in the ministry of the Word. He served in various parts of his country. His charming daughter was sent to London to study music. This fine girl studied faithfully.

Then her father passed away. A telegram was sent to Dr. A. C. Dixon, pastor of the Metropolitan Tabernacle in London, asking him to inform the girl that her father had died.

When Dr. Dixon told her, at first her grief brought no tears. Finally she broke into weeping and said, "I was here in London only because Daddy wanted me to be. He loved music. I was toiling so hard so I could return home and play especially well for him. All I have lived for during these months was just to please my father!"

This, my friend, should be the desire of all—to please God. Jesus said of His earthly ministry, "I do always those things that please him" (John 8:29).

• • • •

"SOMEONE I COULD NOT SEE TURNED ME IN THE RIGHT DIRECTION"

In his testimony, a man told about a victory in his life.

He had tuberculosis when he was seventeen years old. Hoping to ease his pain, he began to drink. At age twenty-five he was an alcoholic.

After becoming a Christian, he quit drinking. Two years after his conversion, he told this story:

> I went to bed last night after reading the Bible, thanking God for the day's victory, and asking Him to take me through the night.
>
> I woke up past midnight and had the old urge to drink. I got out of bed, dressed, and was in my car driving like a man who has a brain above a brain, a will above a will. Twenty miles from home I came to the crossroads that would lead me into the hills where I used to buy liquor. Suddenly I realized Someone was in the car with me, Someone I couldn't see. He helped me brake the car and turn it around. He helped me drive

the twenty miles back home. He gave me His blessing at the door, then was gone.

Thank God that Jesus feels, understands, and has compassion on His children and also on a lost, unregenerate world.

••••

YOU CAN'T LIVE AS YOU PLEASE AND NOT FACE YOUR DEEDS

An article appeared in the *Christian Herald* magazine entitled "It's My Life, Isn't It?"

It told about a twenty-one-year-old college student who was gently reproved by one of his professors for doing certain things.

The professor asked the young man, "Why do you run the risk of smoking?"

"It is really up to me, isn't it? It is my lungs, my health, my life, isn't it?"

The professor quizzed him about his use of marijuana, whiskey, etc.

"It is my life; I can do as I please."

The professor asked, "What about driving dangerously, say, a hundred miles per hour?"

"It is okay on an empty road with no passengers. See what I mean?"

Every question asked got a similar response.

This young man is an example of multitudes who think they can live as they please and not have to face a righteous God. That is not so. You will give an account of your deeds at the great white throne judgment when you stand before God. Remember also in this world you have an influence for good or for evil.

••••

WHAT'S WRONG WITH US?

A pastor raised the question in a gathering of ministers, "What's wrong with us anyway? We just don't seem to be doing much for Christ."

Thinking upon this, another preacher in the meeting wrote the following list:

We are lazy and weak.

We are selfish and unconcerned about others.

We love and worship money.

We are idol worshipers, having many gods.

We have depraved and defiled womanhood by glorifying sex.

We have failed to teach and correct our children.

We teach our children everything but good sense and the Bible.

We have torn down and thrown away the family altar.

We enjoy self-pity and pamper ourselves.

We are pleasure mad.

We are a nation of liars.

We make a mockery of God by rejecting His teachings and calling ourselves Christians.

We are blind to truth and nibble at any bait that the Devil dangles before us.

We are fiddling and fooling while America burns.

●●●●

MR. MOODY'S REPLY

While D. L. Moody was holding meetings in Philadelphia, a lady came to him one day at the close of a service and said, "Mr. Moody, I don't like you."

"Why?"

"Because you are so narrow."

"Why do you think I'm narrow?"

"Because you don't believe in dancing, nor in playing cards, nor in going to the theater, nor in anything I attend."

Mr. Moody replied, "Lady, I can go to the theater whenever I want to."

"What!" she exclaimed. "You can go to the theater whenever you want to? Then I do like you, Mr. Moody! You are much broader than I thought."

Mr. Moody was quick to reply, "Yes, I can go to the theater whenever I want to, but I never want to!"

• • • •

"YOU CANNOT HEAR GEORGE MATHESON AND LIVE IN A CELLAR"

George Matheson wrote the song, "O Love That Wilt Not Let Me Go."

A woman of the slums attending George Matheson's congregation came to know the Gospel's power and was saved by the grace of God. She had long lived in a cellar.

One day her neighbors saw her moving to a new lodging in a sunny apartment. When some acquaintances asked her a few questions, she simply answered, "You cannot hear George Matheson and live in a cellar."

We know what she meant. She had been brought to the Lord through the preaching of George Matheson. Having Christ in her heart made her want to live a higher and nobler life.

• • • •

WHAT MAY SEEM FUTILE ISN'T NECESSARILY SO!

A little boy had made a boat, and he went off in high glee to sail it on the water. The water soon carried it out beyond his reach. In his distress he appealed to a big boy nearby for help: "Will you get it back for me?"

Saying nothing, the older boy picked up a few stones and seemingly was throwing them at the boat. The little fellow thought now his boat was gone; that instead of helping him, the other boy was just ignoring him. Presently he noticed that, instead of hitting the boat, each stone fell beyond it, making a little wave, which moved the boat nearer to shore. Every throw of a stone was planned.

When at last the little boat was brought within reach, how happy the boat owner was! Now he was in possession of his treasure once again!

Sometimes some things in our lives seem very annoying and without sense or plan. If we will commit the matter to the Lord and quietly wait on Him, He will work our problems out for our good and His own glory.

••••

BEWARE! THE MOST USEFUL LIFE CAN SUFFER DEFEAT

An outstanding civic man had a glorious conversion. He was well known and fluent both in speech and with pen. His testimony before large assemblies was very effective.

He was once invited to go to a number of foreign countries with an outstanding evangelist. He went along to write up the meetings. In the course of his trip, he gave his testimony, and many were blessed. In the very midst of the fire of personal victory, he was enticed to strong drink. He became inebriated and was sent back from the evangelistic tour with a shadow upon his life.

I knew this man well. Out of a life of victory, he came to a life of defeat. Since people everywhere knew about this outstanding man's failure, he never regained the place he once held.

I give this illustration just to warn everyone: When you are in the midst of the fire of personal victory, beware! It is then that the viper attacks and ruins a life.

••••

"THAT WORD 'STRENGTHENETH' SAVED ME"

In the midst of our battles of life, I assure you that we can have peace.

It was a stormy night when Oliver Cromwell lay dying. The wind howled, the house shook, and it seemed it would break apart. The great, old, rugged Cromwell said to a loved one near him, "Read to me from Paul's letter to the Philippians." His loved one began to read chapter 4.

When he came to verse 13, "I can do all things through Christ which strengtheneth me," Cromwell said, "Stop right there! When my son died, that word 'strengtheneth' saved me. When my heart was broken, that was the word that saved me. When sorrow swept down on our home as a black vulture, that word 'strengtheneth' saved me. When in one short hour my sun was hid in midnight darkness, that was the word that saved me.

"I can do all things through Christ which **strengtheneth** *me."*

••••

WHAT DOES LIFE MEAN TO YOU?

Here are the replies of a few who answered the question, "What does life mean to you?"

Mary Roberts Rhinehart: "A little work, a little sleep, a little love, and it's all over!"

Edmund Cook: "This life is a hollow bubble!"

Voltaire: "We never live. We are always in the expectation of living."

Colton: "Life is the jailer of the soul in this filthy prison, and its only deliverer is Death!"

Downing: "Life is an empty dream."

Shakespeare: "Life is a walking shadow."

R. Campbell: "Life is a dusty corridor shut at both ends."

Rivaroli: "Life is reasoning of the past, complaining of the present, and trembling for the future!"

How totally different was the reply of the Apostle Paul: "For to me to live is Christ." Paul's joy and strength came from the Saviour. Jesus was the center of his heart's adoration.

•••

LOOK UP IN SPITE OF YOUR TRIALS

Some sickness or weakness of body may be allowed so our Saviour can use us in a greater way. It may be that by our illnesses we are drawn closer to His side and thereby receive more of His power.

It was Charles Haddon Spurgeon who said:

> We learn more true divinity by our trials than by our books. The great reformer said, "Prayer is the best book in my library." He might have added affliction as the next. Sickness is the best doctor of divinity in all the world, and trial is the finest exposition of Scripture.

When Dr. Payson was suffering his last illness, a friend came into his sickroom and said, "I'm sorry to see you lying here on your back."

Dr. Payson answered, "Do you not know why God puts us on our backs?"

"No," was the answer.

Payson said, "In order that we may look upward."

May we not fail to live true to Him whatever the trial He sends. Keep your testimony sure and stedfast. Look upward!

••••

FREE (ONION) BUTTER

I lived at one time with my folks on a twenty-five acre farm not far from the edge of Louisville. The land was beautiful and fertile, but it was afflicted with one grievous pest—wild onions.

It was my job to milk four cows in the morning and night

and then carry the milk to the house, put it in big crocks, and place it in the old-fashioned icebox. When the cream rose to the top, we would skim it off and put the cream into a special jar. At a certain time, I would place the cream into the old-fashioned churn and would churn and churn until the butter came. The butter was molded in the old-fashioned butter molds and then placed in the icebox to get cold and hard.

Many of our kinfolks would come out from Louisville on Sunday for a fine dinner and a few of the products of the farm. I can still see them at the table. My mother would bring out a beautiful, big pound of butter; it would be hard and cold, rocking on the dish. Our kinfolks would spread out the biscuits and cornbread, cut off a big slice of butter, and put it on the bread—all the while talking about how wonderful to live on the farm and have butter free. (Free indeed! I milked, fed and watered the cows. I churned the butter—and they called it free!)

I can still see the kinfolks. They would spread the butter on the bread. After a speech about how fine it was to have *free* butter, they would take great big bites of their biscuits. Then without saying a word, they would quietly slip them down to the edges of their plates and would rarely touch them again. You know what was wrong? Onions! They couldn't stand them. Back on the farm we had onion butter and onion milk until I thought that all milk and butter tasted the same way.

You know, there was something about the onions on the farm. We plowed the ground, and we subsoiled the earth. We burned the face of the earth. We did everything to kill the onions, but they still lived on. We checked with the University of Kentucky to see if they had a plan to kill the onions. They wrote back and said, "We have no plan, but if you find one, please tell us." When I left the farm and went away to school, we still had the finest crop of onions of anybody in the state of Kentucky.

LOVE

BASE ASSURANCE ON GOD'S LOVE

In the book *Our Daily Bread* is the story of a man, a professing Christian who became very ill. In his weakened condition he began to doubt his salvation. He was especially troubled by his lack of love for God. He spoke of this lack to a friend who came to see him.

His friend, a wise counselor and far along on the Christian journey, answered him as follows:

> When I go home from here, I expect to take my baby on my knee, look into her eyes, and listen to her talk. Tired as I am, her presence will rest me.
>
> She, however, loves me but little. If my heart were breaking, it would not disturb her innocent sleep. If my body were racked with pain, it would not interrupt her play. Even if I were to die, she would probably forget me in a few days.
>
> Besides, she never brought me a penny but is a constant expense to me. I am not rich, but there is not enough money in the world to buy my baby. Why is this? Does she love me, or do I love her? Do I withhold my love until I know she loves me? Am I waiting for her to do something worthy of my love before extending it?

This pointed illustration concerning the love of God for His children caused tears to roll down the face of the sick man. "Oh, I see," he exclaimed. "It is not my love for God but God's love for me that I should be thinking of and on which I should base my assurance."

••••

THE SUBSTITUTIONARY DEATH SHOWS CHRIST'S GREAT LOVE

Chinese evangelist Leland Wang has visited Highland Park Baptist Church. He told us of something that happened in his childhood which illustrates the substitutionary work of Christ.

On one occasion, after he had been very naughty, his mother, with a stick in her hand, called him in to be punished. Instead of coming to her, he started to run away, taunting his mother to catch him.

With little chance of catching her small, lively son, she stood still and, within his hearing, said, "I feel ashamed of myself that I brought up a boy who is not willing to be disciplined by his mother when he does wrong; so I must punish myself." Then she began to whip her bare arm.

This so touched Leland's heart that he ran back to her, threw himself into her arms, and pleaded with her not to hurt herself but to punish him; but no further punishment was necessary.

Mr. Wang said that as he grew older, the remembrance of this incident helped him to understand the great love of the Lord Jesus Christ who willingly took our place on the cross.

••••

GOD REWARDS THOSE WHO "GIVE A CUP OF COLD WATER" IN HIS NAME

During a severe battle, two wounded soldiers were awaiting the arrival of an ambulance. The most seriously injured one, who was "going west" more rapidly than the other, said to the other, "Buddy, I'm cold!" His friend, himself in extreme pain and weakness and barely able to move, took off his coat and wrapped it around his dying comrade.

When the ambulance arrived, the first soldier had died, and the other was taken to the hospital and made as comfortable as possible. The nurse heard him say in almost a whisper, "Look, He's coming!" The words died out as he lay quietly a few moments. Again he opened his eyes and, raising his voice slightly, said, "Look, He's coming! He's coming!"

He sank back on the pillow, his strength all but gone. Finally, with extreme effort, he raised himself on his elbow and, with arm outstretched and eyes looking eagerly into the distance, he again cried out, "Look, He's coming! It's Jesus! and He's got on my old coat!"

Love will cause us to give. Love will help us see the lost and dying, then help us do all we can to win them.

••••

GOD'S LOVE—AND MAN'S KINDNESS—DID IT!

When a motherless girl was brought to a reform school, she was angry with all the matrons and refused to obey any orders.

The head matron instructed, "Put her in the room." Hearing this, she visualized a dark room in a dingy basement.

She was taken to the elevator under resistance; but instead of going down on the elevator, she was taken up. She was put in a special room on the top floor—not dark and dreary but a beautiful, sunlit room filled with lovely flowers and the chirping of birds.

The girl looked all around, then began to weep, saying, "I'm sorry that I've been so bad. If my mother had lived, it would have been different."

Soon the matron came up, put her arms around the girl, told her about God's love, and won her to an acceptance of Jesus Christ as Saviour.

••••

WHEN WE TRY AND FAIL, THE
LORD PICKS US UP

A little crippled boy, whose frail legs were covered with steel braces up to his thighs, was hobbling along in a pitiful way, with his mother encouraging him at every step: "That's good! That's fine! Why, you are doing splendidly!" The little fellow would try so hard to do better than he had done, not to show off but to please his mother.

Soon he said, "Mother, watch me. I'm going to run!"

"Very well, darling; let me see you run," she said encouragingly.

A pastor standing nearby was eagerly watching. He saw the crippled boy take two or three steps; then he caught one foot against the brace on his other leg and would have fallen headlong over the curb, had his mother not caught him and put him back on his feet.

She stroked his hair, kissed his pale cheek and said, "That was fine! That was splendid! You can do better next time!"

Oh, my friend, is that not what God does for us? When we try and fail, He picks us up and sends us out to try again.

Thank God for His patience and love toward us!

••••

LOVE FOR A CHILD BROUGHT
LOVE TO A HOUND DOG!

A little fellow had an old dog that was an all-around nuisance to the family, "an abomination to desolation...forever standing where it ought not." The little fellow's soul was knit to his canine friend, and nothing could induce him to get rid of him.

The child became ill. Shortly before he died he said to his loved ones who stood by the bedside: "Take good care of my dog."

Take care of him! From that hour, the worthless hound

was the most precious item in the entire household.

• • • •

THE LONG-SUFFERING SAVIOUR

An atheist challenged God to strike him dead in five minutes. When five minutes passed and he was still alive, he scoffingly said to those about, "What did I tell you?"

A woman standing nearby asked him this: "Sir, have you any children?"

"Yes, why?"

"If one of them handed you a knife and said, 'Daddy, kill me,' would you do it?"

"Why no," replied the astonished man. "I love them too much to do that."

"That is exactly why God did not strike you dead a few moments ago. He loves you too much."

"But God commendeth his love toward us, in that, while we were yet sinners, Christ died for us."—Rom. 5:8.

MISSIONS

DESERVING HELL, YET CHRIST DIED FOR ALL MEN

I have been reading a book entitled *We Two Alone*; it is the story of Irene Farrow and Ruth Hege in the Congo of Africa. These faithful ladies worked under Baptist Mid-Missions serving God with all their hearts.

On January 24, 1964, the communists of the Congo came rushing in and killed Miss Irene Farrow. Her companion missionary, Miss Ruth Hege, was thought by the communists to be dead, but she escaped and wrote the story of what happened.

When I read the account, I was stirred to a great admiration for these courageous missionaries. Then I thought of the savages of the Congo, killing and abusing all they touched. What do they deserve? It seems they deserve nothing better than Hell—but not so! Christ died for everyone, including the savages; and with patience and love, we must keep sending missionaries to do their work and bring the unsaved of the world to the Saviour.

••••

THOUGH DYING, "I MUST GO BACK"

I recently talked with a man who felt called of God to a lonely island off the coast of Alaska. Just a thousand people live there—no electricity, no running water, no doctors, no hospital, not even a drugstore.

This man became a missionary to the Alaskan people when he was past forty years of age. When I met him, he had already spent two years on the field, but because of emphysema, the doctor had ordered him back to this country.

Now he is going back to the mission field. The doctor says he might have two years to live, perhaps not that long.

He said to me, "I must win souls. I must go back and help my people build a church so they can continue on for the Master."

OBEDIENCE

THE ARKANSAS REMEDY

Nearness to Christ will mean obedience. Obedience is going God's way. Obedience is doing what God places before us. Some have to learn that lesson of obedience through stringent experiences. The following story is an example.

On an Arkansas farm a boy was plowing with a mule and a cow hitched to his plow. All went well for awhile, then the mule began kicking. The boy talked to his mule and used his whip on the mule. He might as well have been talking to a stone or whipping the wind.

Then he tried the Arkansas remedy. He took a rope, tied one end to the lower jaw of his balky mule and the other end to the leg doing the kicking. When he gave the signal to start, the mule let go with another mighty kick. That first kick nearly tore off his jaw. The second kick was a little less determined, and there was no third kick. The mule had learned his lesson.

The judgments of God upon us should have the same purpose. God grant that we should learn the foolishness of disobedience and the joy of obeying.

••••

WHEN HE COMMANDS, WE ARE TO OBEY

When just a young woman, Lillian Trotters of England was a very accomplished artist. Sir John Ruskin, one of England's greatest art critics, offered to train Miss Trotters and promised that if she would cooperate with him, he would see that she became one of England's leading painters.

Miss Trotters carefully considered his invitation but turned it down. She wrote in her diary: "I saw that I could not give myself to art in the way that he asked and still seek first the kingdom of God."

Turning her back upon an art career, Miss Trotters went to North Africa to work for Christ among the Moslems.

When we hear His commands, we must obey His voice!

• • • •

SOMETIMES GOD DEALS HARSHLY BUT LOVINGLY

In the realm of courage and faith, I would like to tell you of a gracious couple I met some years ago in Jacksonville, Alabama.

I was conducting services in the First Baptist Church. Night after night I observed a young couple, said to be professors in the state college, bringing many young folks to the services; and many of them were being saved. Everyone rejoiced in what was happening.

One day I was invited to have lunch with this young couple at their home. After the meal they asked if I would sit down in the living room while they talked to me. I did so, and they told their story.

They taught Sunday school classes. They were tithers. They attended every service of the church. When a baby boy came into their home, they decided to divide their time in going to church. They would alternate—one remaining home with the baby and the other going to church. They gave up their Sunday school classes. They put their tithe into the bank to save it for the boy's education.

One day the father announced to his wife that he had resigned his position at the college and they were going to

Nashville where he would work on his Ph.D. degree. They left Jacksonville, went to Nashville and began studying. One day when the father returned home from his classes, his wife met him at the door in tears, tragically disturbed. "O Honey, the baby is seriously ill. Something is drastically wrong."

The professor rushed out of the house and down the street trying to find a doctor. Finally he found a doctor to come to the home. The doctor urged them to get the baby to the hospital at once. They did so, but in a few hours the baby was dead.

The professor said:

> We brought the baby's body back to Jacksonville and buried it in a little cemetery. I brought my wife back to our home. We refused to allow our family or friends to come home with us.
>
> We walked into this living room, knelt down before the settee, and prayed, "Dear Lord, we know why the baby is gone. We turned away from You. We forsook Your side. We stopped going to church, teaching our Sunday school classes, winning souls and tithing. Now the little one is gone.
>
> "We here and now dedicate our lives to Thee and to Thy work."

During the church services, I watched that young couple bring scores of college students to the services. I am sure that in ten days, more than fifty of them accepted Christ as personal Saviour.

● ● ● ●

NOT KEEPING VOW TO GOD COST HIM HIS DAUGHTER

A certain man was under much conviction regarding the needs of his soul and the urgency of publicly acknowledging Christ as his Saviour.

His only child became very sick and finally was at the

point of death. He prayed to God earnestly to restore her to health, promising Him that he would confess Christ and serve Him for the rest of his life if He spared the child.

His daughter did recover, but he "forgot" the promise he had made. Now listen to the tragic end of this true incident.

Shortly afterward, the child was made violently ill by an unknown disease, and almost before they knew what had happened, the little one was taken from them by the icy hand of Death.

The father was prostrate with grief. Yet he realized that God had justly punished him for his delay in accepting Christ and for his broken vow to serve Him.

• • • •

THE JOY TITHING GIVES

Dr. Roy Angel stated that a Christian layman was introduced to a church audience. He was not a handsome man, but gentleness, kindness and happiness were written all over his face. This was his testimony:

> When I was a boy of fourteen, I came home one Saturday with my first pay envelope. Mother and I sat down at the kitchen table, and I poured the money out. There were fourteen one-dollar bills and twenty cents. It was the biggest pile of money I had ever seen!
>
> Mother asked, "What are you going to do with it, Son?"
>
> "I'm going to buy a pair of gloves. Then I want to buy you something, Mother."
>
> "What will you do with the balance, Son?"
>
> "I will start a savings account."
>
> Then with a smile she said, "Aren't you going to give God a tithe?"
>
> "Do I have to?" was my quick response.
>
> After a moment of silence, she answered, "No, Son, it's your money, and you don't have to give God any of

it; but your father and I get a lot of pleasure out of tithing. I feel sure that our tithing has had much to do with the kind of home you have. Suppose you go up to your room and think about it. I would suggest that you pray about it too, then make your own decision."

I stayed upstairs a couple of hours and then went down straight to my mother and asked if she would answer one question for me.

"Certainly. What is it?"

"Suppose I don't tithe. Suppose I don't give God any of it—what would happen to me?"

Soberly she said, "Nothing, Son. Nothing now."

I was greatly relieved. We stood there a moment before I resumed the conversation. "Mama, what will happen if I do tithe?"

Her face was now beaming. "That is just what I wanted you to ask me. The same thing that has happened to your daddy and me. You will find more peace of mind, more joy, more satisfaction in being a good steward than in any one thing that you will ever do. The whole world will be sweeter. You will have joy in your prayer life. You will be proud of your service, and you will know that God is proud of you. You will grow spiritually strong. Your Christianity and your church will be very precious to you.

The speaker stood there a bit choked up, and the hundreds of people in front of him had their emotions deeply stirred. When he could talk again, he said in a husky voice:

You know, it makes me tremble, tremble, tremble, like the old song says, when I think, *Suppose I hadn't started to tithe.* Out of the bottom of my heart I can say that nothing in the world has meant as much to me in my relationship to God as tithing.

How about you? Do you believe what God said—"I will...open you the windows of heaven, and pour you out a blessing, that there shall not be room enough to receive it"?

••••

DANGER IN DELAY!

There is danger in delay!

I am reminded of a man I went to see in Birmingham, Alabama. I could sense that he was not far from the end of his journey. There was a strange odor in the room. The sick man told me what had happened.

Some weeks before, a small drop of acid had fallen upon his leg while he worked in a Birmingham plant. He had put a little salve on the sore but wasn't concerned about it. When the sore became larger, he went to a doctor and was given an inexpensive medication, but the sore kept on increasing in size. He thought that it would eventually go away.

Perhaps it will heal by some of my home remedies, he thought.

However, it didn't heal. The burn had increased until much of his body was affected.

Only a few days after I had visited this man in the hospital, I conducted his funeral. The danger of delay! How tragic that we keep putting things off!

Every sermon should stress the danger of delay! What we do for God, we must do now. Don't wait another day. If you are unsaved, come to Christ today.

PRAISE

DON'T LET YOUR SONG BE SILENCED

A mother was dying. She called her grown children around her bed and said, "Darlings, I'm about to go. I want you to sing me over the river."

They got hymnbooks and, looking into her pale face, asked, "What shall we sing, Mother?" She replied, "There is but one subject! Sing to me of Jesus and His love!"

While they sang, she slipped out into eternity and doubtless listened to the rest of the song from the other side.

Don't let your song be silenced by circumstances. Paul and Silas sang in a prison cell, no doubt a place of filth, foul air and pestilence. Their feet were in the stocks, and doubtless their hands were manacled; but their mouths were open, and their praises flowed out to God.

••••

"GIMME, GIMME, GIMME" WITH NEVER A "THANK YOU"

A street urchin went up to a man and said, "Mister, gimme a nickel."

Said the man, "When I looked at his ragged clothes and dirty face, I said, 'Why, certainly,' and handed him a nickel. He jammed it in his pocket, stuck out his hand and said, 'Gimme another one.' I said, 'You little ingrate! I'll give you the toe of my boot.'"

The man said, "I went on down the street mad as a

hornet; then I thought, *Why did you get so angry with that boy when you have been treating your Heavenly Father that way for years? You have said, "Lord, give me this and give me that"; and when He gave it to you, before thanking Him, you said, "Now, give me something else."*

The man said, "I confessed my sin and asked the Lord to forgive me and promised Him that I would be more grateful."

Are you grateful today for your salvation? Are you praising God for all He has done for you? Do you give Him thanks for food and clothes, health and family?

Oh, how ungrateful to God we can be!

••••

KNOW WHAT YOU ARE SINGING

Years ago when I began studying voice in Louisville, Kentucky, one of my teachers gave me the song entitled "Invictus." I suppose I must have used the song scores of times in rehearsals and in performances, not realizing how empty the words of the song were:

> **Out of the night that covers me,**
> **Black as the Pit from pole to pole,**
> **I thank whatever gods may be**
> **For my unconquerable soul.**
>
> **In the fell clutch of circumstance**
> **I have not winced nor cried aloud.**
> **Under the bludgeonings of chance**
> **My head is bloody, but unbowed.**
>
> **Beyond this place of wrath and tears**
> **Looms but the Horror of the shade,**
> **And yet the menace of the years**
> **Finds, and shall find me unafraid.**
>
> **It matters not how strait the gate,**
> **How charged with punishments the scroll,**

I am the master of my fate;
I am the captain of my soul.

I would a thousand times rather sing:

Jesus is all the world to me,
My life, my joy, my all;
He is my strength from day to day,
Without Him I would fall.

When I am sad to Him I go,
No other one can cheer me so;
When I am sad He makes me glad—
He's my Friend.

PRAYER

QUOTES

"When it seems hardest to pray, pray hardest."

"Prayer will make a man cease from sin—or sin will make a man cease from prayer."

"Prayerless pews make powerless pulpits."

"Let prayer be the key of the day and the bolt of the night."

• • • •

"DR. TRUETT, DO YOU BELIEVE WHAT YOU PREACH?"

When just a young man, the great preacher, George Truett, went to Alabama to conduct a series of revival services. One morning he spoke on the text, "If two of you shall agree on earth as touching any thing that they shall ask, it shall be done for them of my Father."

At the close of the service, an elderly lady asked him if he believed what he had preached. He replied that he did, for it was in the Bible.

The woman said, "Dr. Truett, I mean, do you believe it?"

Again he replied, "My good lady, it is in the Bible. Of course, I believe it."

"Fine," she said, "I have been looking for someone who believes it. It is like this: My husband is seventy years old and is captain on a steamboat on the Mississippi River, and he isn't a Christian. Will you join me in claiming this promise?"

Dr. Truett just stood there. Did he believe it in that way? While he waited, a middle-aged blacksmith stepped around and said, "Auntie, I'll claim it with you." He walked around beside her. The two knelt in the aisle, and as simply as children, they talked to their Father about this need. They claimed the old captain for Jesus Christ.

Dr. Truett said there was real shouting the next morning when this old captain came to church and accepted Christ as his Saviour.

Prayer was effective, and prayer worked!

• • • •

THE ONE WHO ANSWERS PRAYER
MUST BE REVERED

I don't like light and foolish talk about the matter of prayer.

Recently I was visiting a sick person. A former member of our church was there also. When I made some comment about how the sick one was improving, the former member replied, "Yes, the Man upstairs is surely working." I tried to appear innocent, and I asked for a clarification of that statement.

"Oh, you know, the Man upstairs has been good to this person."

I kept on pressing for an explanation. Finally I was told, "Oh, you know, the Man upstairs—He's the One who answers prayer."

I looked that person straight in the eye, and I said, "Never be guilty of saying that again! When you speak of your Heavenly Father, you speak of Him in reverence. You don't call Him 'the Man upstairs.'"

The place of prayer is sacred, and the God who answers must be revered.

• • • •

SWEET HOURS OF PRAYER
ACCOMPLISH MUCH

Adoniram Judson, the missionary who suffered so much in the beginning of his ministry, attributed all his success to the fact that he spent much time in daily prayer. He said:

> Arrange thy affairs, if possible, so that thou canst leisurely devote two or three hours every day, not merely to devotional exercises, but to the very act of secret prayer and communion with God.
>
> Endeavor seven times a day to withdraw from business and company and lift thy soul to God in private retirement. Begin the day by rising after midnight and devoting some time amid the silence of the darkness of the night to this sacred work. Let the hour of opening dawn find thee at the same work. Let the hours of nine, twelve, three, six and nine at night witness the same.

When you read this, you may say, "Impossible. No one could pray this much. There is not time for it."

It isn't impossible if we treat prayer as the greatest business in the world, if we understand that prayers never die, if we realize that men who accomplished much for God spent hours in daily prayer.

••••

OUR FATHER IS WATCHING OVER
US IN EVERY STORM OF LIFE

A ship sailing between Liverpool and New York was caught in a sudden squall of wind that arose at sea. The ship was thrown on her side by the force of the gale, crashing everything movable. The passengers quickly were conscious of great danger.

All on board were alarmed, with the exception of the eight-year-old daughter of the captain.

"What's the matter?" asked the child, rubbing her eyes as she was thrown out of bed.

Her mother told her of the imminent peril.

"Isn't Daddy on deck?"

Informed that he was, she trustfully replied, "Then I'm going back to bed." So saying, she dropped herself on her pillow without a fear in the world. In a few moments she was fast asleep.

Our Father in Heaven is also watching over us in every storm of life. We are safe in His care.

• • • •

"PAPA'S PRAYER STARTED ME ON THE UPWARD WAY"

Dr. George Truett preached one Sunday morning and pleaded with his people to take time to read the Bible and pray with their families. He told them to gather their loved ones together in the evening when the day was done and talk about Christ, read His Word, and plead for His mercy.

One outstanding businessman, whose voice was often heard in the city, searched him out that morning and said, "Dr. Truett, though I have lived miserably and far from what is consistently right, I will turn over a new leaf. We will have family prayer at my house tonight and every night henceforth."

The next morning Dr. Truett was crossing the street and saw the sixteen-year-old son of this businessman coming toward him. The boy was deeply concerned over something, so he asked, "What is it, my boy? What can I do for you?"

"Dr. Truett, you should have been at our house last night."

"What happened at your house?"

"Oh, you should have been there! Papa prayed last night! Papa had someone call Sister and me into the room, and Papa sobbed as he told us he had not lived like a Christian father ought to live. Papa asked Sister and me to forgive him. Neither of us knew what to say. Papa asked Mama to open the Bible for him. He tried to read it but couldn't; he was too broken up. Then Papa knelt down and prayed, mostly for himself. When he got up he said, 'Children, Papa is going to live a different life from this time on.'

"I went to my room and couldn't sleep."

Dr. Truett then asked him, "Why could you not sleep, my boy?"

The young man leaned close to the preacher and said, "I found out last night that I'm a sinner and I'm lost. I've been searching for you all morning. I need to talk to you. Can you tell me what to do?"

They entered a little vacant storehouse. There he told the boy how to be saved. The lad made a simple, honest surrender and was saved on that Monday morning.

The next Sunday the boy came forward in church. Dr. Truett said, "Tell us, my boy, what started you toward Christ?"

The boy looked across at his father on the other side of the church house and said, "Papa's prayer last Sunday night started me on the upward way."

••••

FALSE GODS CANNOT HEAR OR ANSWER THE CRY OF A BROKEN HEART

Two gentlemen standing near a great heathen temple in India saw a native woman approach the temple with a little child in her arms. She lifted the child before the idol, and they saw it was sick and deformed. They heard the woman pray, "Grant that my child may become comely and fair and strong like other children."

When she turned to go away, one of the men approached her and asked, "Friend, to whom were you praying?"

She answered, "I don't know, but surely there must be someone somewhere to hear a mother's cry and keep a mother's heart from breaking."

Such an illustration affords me an opportunity to say there is Someone somewhere—a God who answers prayer. Come to Him with your sick loved one. Don't seek out some heathen idol who cannot hear the cries of a broken heart.

••••

GOD'S CONCERN FOR THE INDIVIDUAL

A young lady in Rossville, Georgia, wrote to me this week concerning the publication of her poems.

"I truly believe that God must have a reason for telling me what to write. I am asking your help because I know He talks to you too."

She enclosed a poem, and the first stanza reads as follows:

> **I know that it sounds strange to some**
> **Each time they hear me say,**
> **"Do you know something wonderful?**
> **God talked to me today!"**

I am not a very good critic of poetry, but I believe what the girl has written—God does talk to us!

Now, if God talked to Joshua, then He will talk to you and me. When God gave His guidance to Joshua, battles were won, and the people of Israel established.

Since God talked to Gideon and gave him directions, then God will talk to us.

Since God talked to Daniel and stood by him in many trying hours, then God will talk to us and stand by us.

Since God talked to Peter, James and John, then He will talk to you and me.

Since God talked to Paul and directed him, then He will do the same for us.

God is interested in you. God is concerned about the individual. He had concern for Nicodemus, for the woman at the well, for the rich young ruler. We also see His concern for Saul of Tarsus on the way to Damascus, for John on the Isle of Patmos, and for so many other individuals in the Bible. This makes me believe He is concerned for us today, for He is no respecter of persons.

Jesus works with the individual. He knows you and your need, and He knows what you can become.

• • • •

NOT ASHAMED TO GIVE THANKS

An old Christian farmer was spending the day in a large city. Entering a restaurant for his noon meal, he found a table near a group of young men. When his meal was served, he bowed his head and quietly gave thanks for the food before him.

The young men observing this thought they would ridicule and embarrass the old gentleman. One called out, "Hey, farmer, does everyone do that where you live?"

The old man looked at the callow youth and said, "No, son, the pigs don't."

• • • •

BE NOT AS THE PHARISEES WHO "FOR A PRETENCE MAKE LONG PRAYERS"

Whenever I hear a public prayer that takes longer than seems wise, I always think of old Brother Bryan of Birmingham, Alabama, one of the best-loved men in the entire city. He preached almost fifty years in the Third Presbyterian Church. His parish took in the whole city. He visited all of the firehalls, the police stations, the factories and the radio stations.

He prayed often and anywhere. He would stop a man on the street, tell him about Jesus, then without hesitation kneel down by the curbstone and pray for him.

Brother Bryan had one characteristic in his old age—he believed in brief public prayers. On one occasion, while attending a funeral, a brother prayed too long. He covered the whole Bible and almost all of the earth. After some time went by, Brother Bryan walked over to him, nudged his side and said, "My dear friend, if you would spend more time in secret prayer, you wouldn't have to pray so long in public."

• • • •

DR. ERNEST REVEAL'S PRAYER

Dr. Ernest Reveal of the Evansville Rescue Mission taught me so much about feeling the presence of our Lord. In his prayer times, he would talk to the Lord like the Lord was seated in the chair opposite him.

I recall reading how one day he was praying about a financial burden for the mission in Evansville. They were having difficulty in getting enough money to pay the bills. The mission had been going for many years, and thousands had come to a knowledge of Jesus Christ.

Strangely enough, he leaned back in his chair with his eyes closed. All over the top of the desk were laid current bills, and he was praying about them. "Lord, I've been adding up these bills. These bills of Yours add up to five hundred dollars. Now these are not my bills—they are Yours. I don't owe anybody anything. Lord, You can do as You please about them; but if You don't pay these bills, there is sure going to be a stink in town!"

Shocked? So was I.

But at ten o'clock the mail came. In it was one check for five hundred dollars, which would pay all the bills spread out on his desk that morning!

I think the Lord was pleased with that kind of praying.

• • • •

"PLEASE RECEIVE HIM AS MYSELF"

The story is told of a man and his son in Indianapolis. During the Civil War the boy enlisted in the Union Army. The father was a banker, and though he consented to his son's going, it seemed as if it would take his very life to see him go.

The father became immensely interested in soldiers. Whenever he saw a uniform, his heart went out to the one wearing it. He thought of his own son. He spent much time with them—to the neglect of his business. He gave his money for raising companies or regiments and for caring for soldiers who came home sick.

At last his friends remonstrated: "There ought to be moderation in all things. You have no right to neglect your business in this manner."

The businessman resolved that he would spend less time and thought on soldiers. He would attend to his business and let the government take care of the boys in blue. After he came to this decision, there stepped into his bank one day a private soldier in a faded, worn uniform. His face and hands showed the marks of the hospitals. The poor fellow was fumbling in his shirt to get something when the banker saw him. Perceiving his purpose, he said to the fellow, "My dear fellow, I cannot do anything for you today, for I am extremely busy. You will have to go up to headquarters. The officers there will look after you."

The poor convalescent stood, not seeming to understand what was said. Still he fumbled in his shirt. At last he fished out a scrap of dirty paper on which there were a few lines written in pencil. He laid this soiled sheet before the banker. On it were written these words:

Dear Father:

This is one of my comrades. He was wounded in our

last fight and has been in the hospital. Please receive him as myself.

Charlie

In a moment, all the resolutions which the banker had made fled away. He took the boy to his palatial home, put him in Charlie's room, and gave him Charlie's seat at the table. He kept him until food and rest and love had brought him back to life, then sent him back to his place of service. His boy asked in the name of a son, and the father responded.

Jesus said, "If ye shall ask any thing in my name, I will do it." We cannot come of ourselves, but in confidence we can come in the name of Jesus and make a request for our needs.

• • • •

PRAYER BROUGHT CALMNESS IN TIME OF DANGER

A medical missionary, captured by bandits in China and informed that he was to be shot at a location ten minutes away, relates how fear and helplessness came over him at the thought of such a death so far from his native country, friends and family. Still he had strength enough to pray, "My Lord God, have mercy on me. Give me strength for this trial. Take away all fear, and if I have to die, let me die like a man."

He said that instantly his terrible fear began to disappear. By the time he had reached the gorge where he was to be shot, he felt perfectly calm and unafraid. At the last moment, the bandits relented, and his life was spared.

In the following days, full of danger and suffering, the memory of this experience was cherished more and more. This is what he said:

My own will had failed in the most critical moment

of my life, but the knowledge that I could depend on a power greater than my own, One that had not failed me in that crisis, sustained me in a wonderful way to the very end of my captivity. What an ingratitude it would be not to proclaim this power!

•••••

MOODY PRAYED; HIS NEED MIRACULOUSLY SUPPLIED!

During the great evangelistic campaign when the World's Fair was in Chicago, D. L. Moody had need of three thousand dollars one day. Things were very pressing, and his need at that time was great. He knelt in his room at the Bible institute in Chicago and prayed, "Lord, You know I must have three thousand dollars today, and I am too busy with Your work to go out and get it. Please send it to me. I thank You. In Jesus' name. Amen."

Mr. Moody rose from the place of prayer and went about his work. He was preaching in his own church auditorium. The audience had assembled; the platform was filled.

A young woman came up to an usher and said, "I wish to see Mr. Moody."

He answered, "You cannot see him now. The meeting is about to begin."

She said, "I must see Mr. Moody."

He again said, "But you cannot see him now."

She went around to another aisle and tried another usher, with the same result. She then went around to the stage entrance, and the usher, thinking her to be a singer, did not detain her. She worked her way down front and put an envelope in Mr. Moody's hand. He crushed it into his vest pocket and went on with his meeting.

At dinner he remembered that he had received that letter at the meeting, took it out of his pocket, and found it to contain a check for three thousand dollars—the answer to his prayer.

He learned afterward that on that morning a Christian woman said to herself, *These are busy days for Mr. Moody. He must require a great deal of money.* She made out a check for one thousand dollars; but after she had written it, the Spirit said to her, "That will not be sufficient. He will need more money than that." She tore the check up and made out another check for two thousand dollars, but she felt sure that it was not sufficient. She destroyed the slip of paper and wrote another check for three thousand dollars. She put it in an envelope and called her maid and said, "Will you please put this in the post office box." Just as the maid was about to leave the room, she said, "He may not get it until tomorrow. He may need it today. Put on your coat, slip over to the auditorium, give it to Mr. Moody, and do not let anyone else have it."

We can come with confidence and pray about our personal needs and know that God will give His definite answer.

•••

SAYING HIS A-B-C'S TO GOD

A man was walking by one of the beautiful hedge rows in England and saw a little lad on his knees. Pausing a moment, he heard him repeating his letters: "A-B-C-D-E-F-G..." The little fellow went clear through the alphabet. When he had finished, he began again: "A-B-C-D..." and on to the end. He continued until he had repeated the alphabet perhaps half a dozen times, after which he said, "Amen."

The gentleman said to the little fellow, "My boy, what have you been doing?"

"I was praying, Sir."

"Praying? But you were only saying letters over and over."

"Yes, I don't know what to ask for, so I thought I would

say the letters to God a good many times and ask Him to put them together the right way for me."

The story has a bit of humor, but it also has the truth. There are times when we don't know how to pray.

I talked to some people who found themselves in such distressing circumstances that they didn't know how to call upon God for specific needs. They lacked wisdom to know how to pray.

PREACHING

"SPEAK A GOOD WORD
FOR JESUS CHRIST"

A poor and humble Scotch mother had an ambition for her only boy to become a minister of the Gospel. To this end she made every sacrifice, denying herself many comforts so she could put him through college when the time came.

After she was taken with a serious illness, the young lad was brought into her presence. She told him of the hope that was in her heart.

Her vision was rapidly dimming. After asking him to follow Christ and meet her in Gloryland, with failing voice she said, "I cannot see you now, John, but I know you are there. I have but one wish. If God calls you to the ministry, do not refuse; and the first day you preach in the church, speak a good word for Jesus Christ. And, John, I will hear you that day, though you'll not see me, and I'll be satisfied." With this she went to be with the Lord.

John was called to preach. He prepared himself for the time when he was to give his first sermon in the First Baptist Church. Being a scholarship man, he felt that some unusual deliverance would be expected by the congregation. While he would be careful and say nothing rash, it was natural that he must state the present position of theological thought; then he might have to quote some of the modern theologians.

He was living with a saintly aunt who had stood with him

at his mother's deathbed and heard her dying request. Noticing the anxious look on her face, he asked, "What are you thinking about, Auntie? Are you afraid of my theology?"

"No, John, it's not that I am afraid of your new views or about your faith. It is not for me to advise you; but I remind you that you will be preaching to just plain country folks. Each has his own temptation, and each is troubled with many cares of the world. They will need a clear word to comfort their hearts and to show them the way to life everlasting. You'll say what's right, no doubt, and I will be pleased with it. But, O laddie, be sure to say a good word for Jesus Christ."

Then came the struggle. The sermon had all been prepared. The brilliant opening, the historic parallel, the review of modern thought, and the trenchant criticism of old-fashioned theology—what else could he say to the people? In the stillness of the room he heard a voice that for five years had been silent on earth, "Speak a good word for Jesus Christ."

The next minute he was kneeling on the hearth and pressing his great sermon into the fire. He saw the words shrivel and disappear. When the last black piece fluttered out of sight, he could see his mother's face again; but this time her eyes were smiling, and there was peace.

He went into the pulpit the next morning. One who sat in the pew said, "I never saw Jesus Christ more plainly and never realized the unseen world so vividly as I did that day in the church when the boy preached."

• • • •

FIVE HUNDRED SAVED IN ONE DAY!

Elijah Kimsey, a very effective mountain evangelist, was a great uncle of Dr. George W. Truett.

In Clay County, North Carolina, they were having a tent

meeting. It had been going on for about a week, but no one had been saved. Then one morning Elijah Kimsey came before the pastors and stated, "I have prayed all night. God has laid on my heart to preach. I come before you requesting that you permit me to preach."

The pastors knew him and believed in him. They said, "All right, we have four preaching hours—at 8:00 a.m., 11:30 a.m., 4:00 p.m. and 7:00 p.m. Which hour do you want?"

"The sooner, the better for me."

They gave him the 8:00 a.m. hour, and he began preaching. The power of God came on them. Uncle Elijah, as he was known, was one moment in the pulpit preaching, the next, walking in the aisles. At one moment he was speaking personally to an unsaved one; the next, kneeling by the side of a friend.

News of the service went out through the mountain coves and across the mountaintops. People came in oxcarts, walking, riding—any way they could get there.

The services didn't close for the eleven o'clock hour nor for the four o'clock hour nor for the seven o'clock hour. It seemed that no one ever knew at what hour in the night the service was over.

That day five hundred men, women and young people gave their hearts to the Lord Jesus Christ! Some people say that the service meant more to that section of the country than anything else that had ever happened.

We see here what one man who is filled with the Holy Spirit can do for God.

• • • •

AN EXAMPLE OF WASTED TIME

Paul, the Fundamentalist;
Paul, the Great Preacher of the Word of God;
Paul, Who Had Such a Calling to Preach That

He Had No Time for Anything Else

Someone placed a clipping in my hand telling of the pastor of a First Presbyterian Church who has just co-authored with his uncle a book on pocket billiards, *Cue Tips*.

The idea for writing the book came from the uncle. Knowing that his nephew was a great pool player and was also a four-year pool champion in college, he brought his nephew into the book; hence they co-authored a volume on playing pool.

I wonder if you could imagine the Apostle Paul's having time for this kind of foolishness!

REVIVAL

EVAN ROBERTS' MESSAGE
TO AMERICA

The book entitled *When the Fire Fell* tells of the great revivals under the leadership of Evan Roberts. This young man was greatly used of God. He was not a mighty preacher, but he was a tremendous Christian.

A friend from America, visiting the revival in South Wales, asked Mr. Roberts for some message he could take back to America. This is what the young man said:

> The prophecy of Joel is being fulfilled. The Lord says, "I will pour out my spirit upon all flesh." Since that is so, then all flesh must be prepared to receive the Spirit.
>
> First, clear all the past, with every sin confessed to God, and any wrong to man righted.
>
> Secondly, remove once and for all out of our lives every doubtful thing.
>
> Thirdly, be obedient, prompt and implicit when the Holy Spirit speaks.
>
> Fourth, a public confession of Jesus Christ. For Christ said, "If I be lifted up...will draw all men unto me."

That is it! If we know Christ ourselves, then we should witness for Him.

●●●●

NEEDING SPIRITUAL WARMTH

It is an old story but one that still has meaning. A church was destroyed by fire. A great crowd of spectators gathered, as is usually the case. Among them was a man known to be a skeptic. One of the church members could not refrain from remarking to him, "I never saw you near the church before."

"No," replied the skeptic; "but then, I never saw the church on fire before."

SALVATION

BOOTBLACK BECAME RENOWNED PULPIT ORATOR

A little boy lived in Oxford, and his job was to clean the boots of the students at that famous university.

The boy was poor but brilliant. His task was menial, but he considered it "holy ground." He did what he was supposed to do with all his might that his Saviour might be glorified through his efforts.

This lad whose name was George grew rapidly in favor with the students. His prompt and hardy way of doing things and his industrious habits and faithful deeds won their admiration. They saw in him a man of promise. "A boy who can blacken boots that well will study well; he can also be depended upon for other things."

They began teaching him a little each day. Even though he could not afford the expense of actually attending the school, George, eager to learn, accepted their help and surpised all his teachers by his rapid progress.

We cannot begin to tell you of the patience and perseverance of this young man. He went on from step to step, considering all of his life "holy ground."

He soon became a great and learned preacher of the Gospel. He had a burning zeal and a passion for souls, and because of his efforts, thousands came to know Christ.

Thus, a bootblack became the renowned pulpit orator, George Whitefield.

"Study to shew thyself approved unto God, a workman that needeth not to be ashamed, rightly dividing the word of truth."— I Tim. 2:15.

••••

"I'VE BEEN WAITING THIRTY YEARS"

A. C. Dixon told about a New York pastor who became anxious about a certain banker, a member of his congregation to whom he had never spoken directly.

One day he went to the banker's office and asked for a ten-minute interview.

"Have you come on business, Pastor?"

"Yes—business for God and for eternity. I would like to talk to you about your soul."

To the pastor's surprise, the banker replied, "I've been waiting thirty years for someone to tell me how to get saved. Ten minutes, you say? Come to my house and make it the whole evening."

At the home the pastor led the banker to Christ and salvation.

Souls are still hungry for the Gospel—even a banker. Oh, let us be faithful to witness to and win them!

••••

EIGHTY, BUT TWO

Rowland Hill, the evangelist, said one day he saw on the street a man who must have been in his eighties, and he felt impressed to ask him his age. The man looked at him, tried to speak, but his voice broke. In tears he finally answered, "I am two years old."

The astonished Mr. Hill said, "Two years old?"

"Yes. I never lived until two years ago; that's when I met Christ and received Him as my Saviour."

••••

"NOW!"

Thomas Chalmers, a great Scottish preacher, stopped in the midst of a sermon and, flinging his arm out with index finger pointed straight at a noted judge who sat at the rear of the auditorium, cried, "Judge, God says, 'Now.' Satan says, 'Some other time.' What do you say?"

The judge rose to his feet and with trembling voice declared, "I have resisted the voice of God too long. I have compromised, put off doing what I should already have done, but I now yield myself to God. I say with Him, 'Now!'"

••••

NOTHING TO HOLD ONTO

The late General William Booth told of a family of four who lived in London—the mother, the father, a son and a daughter—all avowed enemies of the Gospel of Christ. So antagonistic were they that they declared they never wanted a Christian to enter their home.

In the community was a young lady who yearned and prayed for their salvation. When she heard that the son was sick, she decided to visit them in spite of their opposition.

She climbed the stairs and paused for breath just outside the apartment door. Then she heard the voice of the father: "Hold on, Son, hold on. You may die, but there's nothing beyond. We have read all the books, reasoned it out. There is nothing beyond. Soon you will drift off into peaceful sleep, and that will be all. Hold on, Son."

Then the visiting girl heard the sobbing cry of the mother: "My precious boy, it breaks my heart to see you go, but don't be afraid. We have investigated all possibilities of the future life, and there is nothing out there. You will soon be asleep forever. Hold on, Son, hold on."

Then she heard the sister say, "Don't falter now, Brother. You know that we decided a long time ago there is nothing beyond death. Soon you will go to sleep, and that will be all. Just hold on."

Then she heard the voice of the boy, laden with despair and grief: "That's all right, but there is nothing to hold onto. I am going out into the dark with nothing to hold onto."

That is right—nothing for the one who does not have Christ. Without Jesus, you are of all men most miserable.

How sad is the destitution of a life without the Saviour! Thanks be unto God, that need not happen to you. You can be saved now. If you will repent and believe on the Lord Jesus Christ, salvation will be yours. Then you will have something to hold onto—an anchor that will hold fast.

• • • •

"THAT SUN IS JUST ABOUT DOWN"

A few days ago I had called upon a number of the residents at our beautiful rest home in Chattanooga. As I started out the front door to leave, I saw a man standing at the window looking to the west. He was weak, so both hands were resting upon the glass. As I came to the door, he turned to me and said, "The sun is just about down." Of course, you and I know what he meant.

When I got in my car to drive away, I thought of the dear man, advanced in years, weak in body, watching the setting sun.

This week I had a funeral service for a young man thirty-two years old. Tomorrow may be the Home-going for someone twice or three times that age.

It is my concern that all those watching the setting sun have Christ in their hearts and peace in their souls. All who have trusted Him as their Saviour can have this peace and reassurance. Those who haven't trusted Christ can do so right now.

• • • •

"THIS IS REAL LIVING!"

Some years ago a poor, drunken bum staggered into our downtown mission in Chattanooga. It looked as though he had come to the end of the way. Strong drink had ruined his body and mind. His home had been wrecked; his wife had divorced him and taken their son with her; but this man heard the Gospel, was saved, and I baptized him.

Shortly after his salvation, he left Chattanooga. A year or so after his experience of salvation I saw him again in another city. He reminded me, "I am the drunken bum who was saved at your mission, and you baptized me!"

Now the man was clean and looked very handsome. A lady was at his side. "This is my wife," he said. Then a fine boy of twelve stepped up, and he said, "This is my son."

He then told me of the miracles God had wrought in his life. After his salvation, he returned home, located his wife, remarried, and started a new business, in which he was quite successful in just a brief time.

With justifiable pride, he stated proudly, "This is real living!"

••••

WE NEVER KNOW WHAT MAY HAPPEN WHEN A YOUNG PERSON ACCEPTS CHRIST

I was recently reading about a revival meeting conducted in a small Baptist church. In the opening days of the meeting, it rained night and day. Because of the mud and high water, very few people could get to church.

The evangelist said, "I suppose we might as well close the meeting. The weather is so bad that the people can't come."

However, the pastor said, "No. We announced this meeting for many months. We prayed for it, and we will continue on."

They went on in spite of the rain, mud, slush and low

attendance. The evangelist was discouraged, but the pastor kept on insisting that they go ahead.

On the last Saturday night, when the evangelist stood up to give his message, three young men came in the door and sat down at the rear of the building. After the sermon the evangelist began his invitation.

One of the dear men of the church went to talk to one of the boys standing at the rear of the building. The young man shook his head and refused to move. In a few moments, though, he left his place and came rushing to the front, accepting Christ as his Saviour. He was followed by another young man; then a little girl accepted Christ.

In two weeks, there were only three professions of faith. Many times the evangelist thought the meeting was a failure. That first young man who led the way on that Saturday evening was Fred F. Brown, for many years pastor of the First Baptist Church of Knoxville, Tennessee. He was a fine scholar, a great pastor and a great soul winner.

When one gets saved, we never know what may happen to his life. All of us hear of such workings of God in young lives. Be faithful to preach the Word.

••••

UGLY SCENERY BECOMES AN ANGEL

I am thinking now of a simple little story that comes out of a village built in the mountains in Europe. When strangers came to the village, they went to view the beautiful scenery. When they came near the place where the beauty could be best viewed, there was always an unsightly scene.

The villagers said, "Between us and our wonderful scenery lies a large, rugged and unsightly boulder. You must be blindfolded until you pass it so your vision of the beautiful scenery will not be marred by the unsightliness of the rock."

One day a visitor came who refused to be blindfolded. While the villagers talked of the mountains, he looked at the boulder. While they spoke of the broad expanse of the fields, he surveyed the surface of the unsightly rock.

Finally he drew away from them and returned to the village. When he came again, it was with a ladder and a kit of tools. He laid the ladder against the face of the rock, then with mallet and chisel, began to cut away the ugly stone. Day after day he labored until the blackness and dirt and ugliness of the long offending boulder were hewn away, and in its place stood the outstretched wings of an angel in virgin whiteness.

From that day to this, it is said the villagers never ask, "Have you seen our scenery?" Instead they ask, "Have you seen our angel?"

That little illustration simply points out that when the Son of God comes into the heart, He transforms man, and his sin, though as scarlet, becomes white like snow. He produces not an angel but something far better: He makes a man into a child of God.

••••

THE ROBBER CHIEFTAIN SAVED

Kazainak, the robber chieftain of Greenland, came to a cabin where a missionary was translating the Gospel of John. When Kazainak asked what he was doing, the missionary told him he was making letters, and with letters, words were made, and that by the use of those words, the Book he had before him could speak.

Kazainak thought that was very wonderful and asked if the Book might speak to him. When the missionary read the story of Christ's sufferings and His death on the cross, the robber chieftain immediately said, "What has this man done? Has he robbed anyone? Has he murdered anyone?"

"No," was the reply. "He has robbed no one, murdered no one; He has done nothing wrong."

"Then why does He suffer? Why does He die?" asked the puzzled robber chieftain.

Then the missionary told him the story of the cross, the story of the atonement, and the meaning of the sufferings of Jesus. When he finished, the hardhearted man was weeping as a child and turned to Christ for salvation.

Christ died for your sins. He paid the price on Calvary's cross. Like the chieftain, you can be saved right where you are. Christ will come into your heart just as He came into Kazainak's heart.

••••

CHURCH MEMBER BUT LOST

Mrs. Jack Stone had been a church member for years and had taught the young ladies' class at the First Baptist Church of Fairfield, Alabama. She had lived an exemplary life. Not only was she a church leader but also a civic leader and president of the Parent-Teachers Association. She was also a college graduate.

Then came that momentous night when she discovered that she was lost and Hell-bound. Long before daybreak, she pounded on the door of our home on Carnegie Avenue. When I went to the door, she fell upon the floor in the living room and said, "I am lost! I want to be saved!"

My wife came into the room, and in a few moments, after reading the Word of God and having prayer, Mrs. Stone accepted Christ as her Saviour.

She was active in church and had Bible knowledge, but she was lost. Then when she saw the danger of being without Christ, she turned to Christ and discovered the reality of salvation.

••••

SINGING "SAVED, SAVED!" WITHOUT SALVATION

I cannot forget one of my great experiences in a revival meeting in Akron, Ohio.

A young man sang "Saved, Saved!" at the beginning of the service in his beautiful tenor voice. I complimented the song. He sat down on the front row.

During my message, I observed how intently he was listening. When I gave the invitation, he left his seat, came toward me and said, "Dr. Roberson, I want to accept Jesus Christ as my personal Saviour."

I began at once to question him regarding this. He said, "I was brought up in the home of a Presbyterian preacher. My father was a minister. I have heard the Gospel again and again. I lived in a home where the Bible was read, but I have never before accepted Christ as my Savior."

That evening Bill Simpson received Christ into his heart.

At the end of the service, I asked him to sing again "Saved, Saved!" He did so with great dignity and with power.

What had been wrong? He was near to salvation, but he had missed the big step of accepting Christ as his Saviour.

• • • •

THE HUNGRY-HEARTED TEN

Many have heard me tell what happened in Haleyville, Alabama, the night I preached on one word, "Condemned," and many were saved.

I was in my hotel room; after eleven o'clock there came a knock at the door. When I opened it, two young men were standing there. A tall lad with red hair asked if he could speak to me. I invited them in. He said, "I would rather talk to you in the lobby."

I went down to the lobby of the hotel with them and found there ten young men. The spokesman of the group said, "We want to know if it is true what you said tonight—that every person outside of Christ is lost forever, condemned already, and bound for Hell."

I repeated some of what I had said in my message and then read John 3:18: "He that believeth not is condemned already." They nodded their heads in agreement, for these lads would not dispute the Word of God.

Then I asked, "Is that as much as you want? Wouldn't you rather have more than this knowledge that a man is lost without Christ?" Quietly they agreed. They would like to know more.

I read more verses from the Bible, then asked them to kneel with me in prayer. After the prayer, I turned to the young spokesman and asked, "Will you here and now accept Christ as your Saviour?" Not just this one, but every young man there, accepted Christ as his Saviour!

I thought it seemed too easy, so I urged them to come forward in the church the next evening and make a public profession of their faith.

The next night I looked for the crowd, but I didn't see them at first. Later I saw them standing in the back rows of the balcony. When we sang the invitation song, there was no response from them during the first verse. I urged people to come forward if they were trusting the Saviour. Then from the balcony all of these young men came to the front to confess that they were accepting Jesus Christ as personal Saviour. Eight united with the Baptist church where I was holding the revival campaign.

••••

LOST CHURCH PIANIST GOT SAVED

I cannot forget the revival meeting I conducted in a northern church. I preached my sermon, gave an invitation, and the audience was singing when suddenly there came a terrible discordant sound from the piano. I turned toward the instrument and saw the pianist bent over upon the keyboard with her head in her arms.

I went to her and asked what troubled her. She answered, "I'm lost. I have never been saved. I've been a church member all my life, but I have never accepted Jesus Christ as my personal Saviour."

To the praise and glory of God, she got saved that night!

••••

THE ONE WHO HAS POWER TO SAVE

Joseph Parker said that the thief on the cross proved to be one of the greatest men who ever lived.

On the cross there was no outward indication of His Lordship; there was no insignia of royalty. Jesus was a captive, condemned, insulted, crucified; yet the dying thief saw Him as a King and as a Redeemer. His words were, "Lord, remember me when thou comest into thy kingdom."

There were no royal robes on Christ, no throne. He was hanging upon a shameful cross, yet the dying thief had faith to recognize Him as the King, One with power to confer royal gifts. This guilty sinner saw in Christ the One with power to save his soul.

The jailer in Philippi found out the same thing on that eventful night when Paul and Silas sang in the prison. He came and heard the message of salvation and believed in the Lord Jesus Christ.

The same was true of Zacchaeus, that proud and haughty tax collector. When pride was stripped away, he looked to Jesus and was saved.

••••

NO BLOOD, NO SALVATION

Some people despise the message of the cross, despise the

Word of God and the way of salvation through Jesus Christ.

R. A. Torrey was holding meetings in the Royal Albert Hall in London. Someone took a hymnbook, went through it, cut out every reference to the blood, then sent it to Dr. Torrey through the mail, saying, "I have gone through your hymnbook and cut out every reference to the blood. Now, sing your songs with the blood left out, and there will be some sense to them."

Dr. Torrey later said, "If any of you should take your Bible, go through it that way, and cut out of both Old and New Testaments every passage referring to the death of Christ or to His atoning blood, you would have only a sadly torn and tattered and useless Bible left—a Bible without a heart and a Gospel without saving power."

The death of Jesus Christ is mentioned some 175 times in the New Testament alone. Besides, there are many prophetic and typical references to the death of Christ in the Old Testament.

What can wash away our sins? *Nothing* but the blood of Jesus! It's the blood, the blood, the blood!

••••

PEACE IN THE PARDON

A man in England was being tried on a serious charge. The lawyer had proved his case. The condemned remained calm.

The jury returned a verdict of guilty. He remained calm.

The judge passed sentence. He remained calm.

Then the one condemned quietly produced the Royal pardon which he had by some means obtained.

There was the secret of his peace! It was not in wealth or health, but in the pardon.

We too can have peace in the pardon which is ours in Jesus Christ our Saviour.

Saved! saved!
My sins are all pardoned, my guilt is all gone!
Saved! saved!
I am saved by the blood of the Crucified One!

There is so much that we cannot understand, but there is one thing we can know: The blood of Christ cleanses us from all sin!

••••

THE COST OF YOUR SALVATION

The king of Ethiopia once took as prisoner a British citizen named Cameron. The Englishman was taken away to a huge stone castle and securely locked in a stone dungeon.

Six months elapsed before the British government found out about the jailed prisoner. They asked the Ethiopian monarch to release him, but their request was denied.

Within ten days, ten thousand English soldiers were aboard ships sailing for Ethiopia. When they landed on the distant shore, they still had to march seven hundred miles under a hot sun in order to free Cameron. By this time, the prisoner had become so weak he had to be carried by stretcher back to safety.

It was computed that this expensive expedition to rescue a single British subject cost some twenty-five million dollars.

My friends, that is an inconceivably small amount when we think of what it cost the Lord to save us from our sins. Christ Jesus, the only begotten Son of God, gave His very life that we might receive our eternal ransom. The Apostle Peter stated,

"Forasmuch as ye know that ye were not redeemed with corruptible things, as silver and gold...

"But with the precious blood of Christ, as of a lamb without blemish and without spot."—I Pet. 1:18, 19.

••••

ONLY THE BLOOD-WASHED
CAN SING REVELATION 1:5

A lady asked the preacher to visit her husband who was gravely ill. After the evangelist had talked to the man awhile, he inquired about his spiritual condition.

"Well," he replied, "I think my chances of getting into Heaven are quite good. I have always been kind to my wife and children, lived a good moral life, and have never intentionally wronged my fellowman."

"That's fine," said the pastor, "but what kind of place do you think Heaven is, and what do you think they do there?"

"Well, I believe there is no sin or sorrow there, and I think they sing a great deal."

Turning to Revelation 1:5, the minister replied, "Yes, they do sing there, and I will read to you one of the songs: 'Unto him that loved us, and washed us from our sins in his own blood'! You see, they are praising the Saviour who loved them and died for them. They have not a word to say about what they have done but only what He has accomplished on their behalf. If you were to go to Heaven on your terms, then one sinner would be there who would never have been cleansed in the precious blood of Christ, and who could not join in this wonderful hymn of praise."

The man's head dropped, and he became silent and thoughtful. After explaining the gospel invitation more fully, the preacher left. The next day when he visited again, the dying man looked up with a light of joy upon his face. "Oh, sir," he exclaimed, "I have received Christ, and now I can sing, 'Unto him that loved us, and washed us from our sins in his own blood.'"

••••

WHAT CHRIST CAN DO TO A LIFE GIVEN TO HIM

Someone asked a highly successful realtor how he made so many sales. The man told his secret.

"Most of the property around here is run down and certainly not attractive. I don't try to sell my prospects a farm as it is. I develop my entire sales plan around the farm that it can be."

He went on to say that he didn't tell a man that the farm had so many acres of bottom land, so many acres of woods, and was so many miles from town. "Instead, I try to show a man what the farm can become."

He studies all about the farm and gives a man three or four ideas of what it could become by careful work. In the prospect's mind, the realtor paints pictures for him. He makes him see the potential of what it could be.

When I read that story, I began to see the thinking of my father when he bought two or three run-down farms around Louisville. The houses were worth nothing; the land was poor; there were no fences, no roads, no walkways—but my dad was a builder. He saw what those farms could become. I am thinking now of how sucessfully he could take a rundown farm and make it into something beautiful.

Ah, my friend, do the same in the work given you. Make a man see what his life can become when he accepts Christ. Make the lost sinner understand that salvation is more than a rescue from Hell. Salvation is life, new life, real life, joyous life—life that supersedes all else.

••••

CHRIST IS KNOCKING; DON'T TURN HIM AWAY

A man gave this illustration:

I once knew of a child who had a rare and serious disease. The distraught parents sought every medical assistance within their reach, but all to no avail.

At last they learned of a doctor in a foreign country who had been successful in the treatment of this unique and usually fatal ailment. They also heard that this specialist was to make a trip to America. In desperation they cabled him to come and help them but received no reply.

Some weeks later, a train passing through a midwestern town developed engine trouble and had to stop for repairs. The famous doctor was on board. Remembering the wire he had received, he left the train in search of the dying patient.

Having found the address, he knocked at the door. When the people saw a bearded stranger who was calling out in a foreign tongue, they decided not to admit him.

Imagine their chagrin and sorrow when they learned by the paper the next day that the man who had sought admittance was the one they so urgently needed! Yet he had been turned away.

Christ is knocking at your heart's door today. Will you open the door and let Him come in? Don't turn Him away!

• • • •

A GIFT, NOT FOR SALE

When Clara Barton was engaged in Red Cross work in Cuba during the Spanish-American War, Theodore Roosevelt came to her to buy some food for the sick and wounded men under his command.

His request was refused. Roosevelt was troubled. He loved his men and was ready to pay for the supplies out of his own pocket.

"How can I get these things?" he asked. "I must have the proper food for my sick men."

"Just ask for it, Colonel," said the surgeon in charge of the Red Cross headquarters.

"Oh," said the Colonel, "then I do ask for it." He got it at once.

Salvation is free. You can't buy it. You must receive it to have it. Salvation is a gift from His hands, a gift without works.

●●●●

ONLY CHRIST CAN MAKE US NEW

Years ago Harry Morehouse was walking in the poor section of a city when he saw a boy about six years of age coming out of a store with a pitcher of milk. The little fellow was making his way carefully down the street when he slipped and fell. The pitcher broke, and milk ran all over the sidewalk.

The child let out a wail, and Morehouse rushed over to see if he was hurt. There was no physical damage, but the youngster would not be consoled. He kept crying over and over, "My mama will whip me. My mama will whip me."

Mr. Morehouse said to him, "Maybe the pitcher is not broken in too many pieces. Let's see if we can put it back together."

The boy stopped crying at once. He watched Mr. Morehouse place the base of the pitcher on the sidewalk and start building up the pieces. There were one or two failures. Each time the boy started crying again, he was silenced by the big preacher.

Finally the whole pitcher was together except for the handle. The preacher handed the piece to the little fellow. He poked it toward where it belonged and knocked the whole thing down again. This time there was no stopping his tears.

He gathered the child in his arms, walked down the street to a nearby store, and bought a new pitcher. Then he and the boy returned to the milk store and had the pitcher washed and filled with milk. He carried the boy in one arm and balanced the pitcher in the other hand until he arrived at the boy's home.

Very gently he deposited the lad on the front steps, put the pitcher carefully into his hands, and asked, "Now will your mama whip you?" The smile broke on the tear-streaked face. "Ah, no sir, because it is a lot better pitcher than we had before."

The illustration is clear. You cannot patch up an old life; Christ has to make you a new person. There is no use trying to patch the pieces together again. Without Christ, we are broken and hopeless and despairing. When we come to Him, He gives us a new nature, a new life. All of this is because of the grace of God.

••••

MAN CANNOT BUILD A LADDER TO HEAVEN!

A newspaper in Sydney, Australia, had this item:

> After collecting more than 300,000 beer bottles for charity in the past ten years, Mrs._____, age seventy-two, of Neutral Bay, is retiring. She has been collecting from 1,000 to 1,500 bottles a week which she puts in bags and sells at about the equivalent of 25¢ a bag. She has raised about $4,000 in this way for charity. She also collects wastepaper for hospitals and rags for spastic centers.
>
> "Now I'll have a bit of time to relax," she said. "I've tried to build a ladder to Heaven."

A poor, lost sinner cannot build a way to Heaven. No one can save himself. Salvation is in Christ Jesus, the Son of God.

••••

"I WILL GIVE YOU THIS IF YOU PROMISE NOT TO PRAY"

Charles Haddon Spurgeon used to tell of the time he heard a young man swear and take the Lord's name in vain. Walking up to him, he touched the blasphemer's arm and said, "Can you pray as well as you can swear?"

The young man laughed and, with a superior air, declared that he had never done anything so useless as praying.

Holding up a coin of considerable worth, Mr. Spurgeon said, "I will give you this if you will promise me never to pray."

Irreverently that young man pocketed the coin with a chuckle.

As the day wore on, he began to feel uneasy. *Never to pray? Never?* Perhaps he had made a bad bargain, for he might need to call upon God someday if he came to an extremity. The more he thought about it, the more he became convinced that he had sold something very precious.

The Holy Spirit's convicting power began softening his heart. When he arrived home that evening, he told his wife of the promise. She was horrified—and rightly so.

"It is true we don't pray," she said, "but someday we may want to."

Talking it over a bit more, the worried couple decided to see if they could find the man who had given the coin and extracted such a promise.

Mr. Spurgeon, who had been hoping for just such a reaction, was soon located. Seeing their deep conviction, he immediately began to deal with them in regard to salvation, and in a short time, both were led to Christ.

••••

$75,000 MEANT MORE THAN
THE SALVATION OF A SOUL

A church put on a drive to raise funds for a new educational plant. They set the goal at $75,000 in cash, to be paid in one month.

The pastor preached a sermon on "Will a Man Rob God?" They took the pledges and the offering. At the close of the service and after counting the money, they had gone far beyond the $75,000.

There was a round of applause. Everyone was hugging and kissing one another. So happy were they that they stood around the church talking for almost an hour.

The next Sunday the preacher preached a good sermon, gave an invitation, and down the aisle came a twelve-year-old boy to accept Christ as Saviour. The pastor said, "I am sure you will want to come and shake hands with this lad and tell him how happy you are that he has accepted Christ."

After the benediction the boy stood at the front all by himself. Eight people came to shake his hand. Raising the $75,000 meant more to them than the salvation of a soul!

I need say no more. You can understand that without further interpretation.

••••

WHERE WERE YOU WHEN
YOU MET CHRIST?

One father met Christ in a most unusual place after rejecting Him for many years. He had closed his mind and heart to every statement of Christ and every offer of salvation.

His young daughter became desperately ill with an incurable disease. Friends urged him to accept Christ as Saviour, but he refused. He laughed at the people and again closed the door on the Son of God.

The daughter passed away. The poor, lost man blamed

God and everyone else for the death of his daughter.

The young daughter had left a paper to be read at her funeral service. It was read by the pastor. It gave such a glowing testimony to the reality of Christ that the lost father left his place, fell down before the casket, and received Christ as his Saviour.

Where were you when you met Christ? It might have been overseas in the armed forces of our country, or it might have been in a hospital when someone introduced you to the Lord Jesus Christ.

It matters not where one is, but it does matter that you turn to Him for salvation. His arms are open wide to receive all who will accept Him as their Saviour.

• • • •

WHAT HAPPENS WHEN ONE IS REDEEMED BY THE GRACE OF GOD?

Let me give another story of success and failure and success again. It comes to me from the late Dr. Ellis Fuller. He told about a prominent lady, a Ph.D. graduate and the dean of women in one of our great southern universities, who came to see him.

"I have lost all my faith, and I am just a drifting, derelict ship. Every time I speak in the name of Christ I condemn myself as being a hypocrite. I cannot stand it any longer. I have made up my mind that I am going to find anchorage for my soul or resign my job. I feel that maybe you can help me. Do you have anything to say? I am in great distress."

Dr. Fuller knew that this educated lady was very troubled. He looked into her face and asked, "Doctor, have you ever been born again? Have you ever been definitely redeemed by the grace of God?"

She answered, "I don't know what you are talking about.

I grew up in the Presbyterian church. We had family prayers. I went to prayer meeting and to the young people's meetings. I have never known anything but just to go to church."

Dr. Fuller said, "But this is different. Have you been born again?"

Then just as simply as possible he told her what he meant. He read to her from the Word of God. He told what it meant to be saved by grace and redeemed by the blood of Jesus Christ.

The woman left. Some time later they met at another great function when Dr. Fuller was the speaker. She came to him at once and said, "Dr. Fuller, I am still on the job, and I am now as much a preacher of the saving grace of God as you are! That is the solution to all my spiritual problems. I have been born again."

••••

"NO MAN CARES FOR MY SOUL"

Some years ago a criminal forfeited his life to the state of Illinois for crimes he had committed. As is the custom, as he sat in the electric chair, he was given the opportunity to say his last words. All he said was, "No man cares about my soul."

The cry of this man is coming from all over the world. Do we care? Do we really care that others hear the message and come to Christ?

Men must hear the Gospel and receive the Lord, or go to Hell. Christ is the only hope for the world and for the individual. Because no one cared, that criminal may be in Hell today; others will be tomorrow.

Let it not be said by any man, "No man careth for my soul."

••••

A LOST CHURCH MEMBER'S LAST CHANCE

A faithful pastor was called to the bedside of an officer of his church. The dying man, in a gasping breath, said, "O Pastor, I have sent for you to tell me how to be saved!"

"What!" asked the pastor. "Is it possible that you have sat under my ministry for these many years and don't know the way of salvation?"

The dying man gasped out, "It is true, Pastor. While you preached, my thoughts were on business. I gave little consideration to what you said. My mind was on the things of the world. Please tell me how to be saved."

Are you saved, my friend? I do not ask if you are a church member. I ask if you are saved. Don't wait until your feet are about to slip into Hell before attending to the most important business in all the world—making sure that you are ready to meet God.

••••

CHRIST THE DOOR; THERE IS NO OTHER ENTRANCE

Recently I read the story of Daniel Currie, a western cattleman. In the last days of his life, he was a great Christian. He had a Christian wife all through the years. He was a fine moral man, liberal with his money, an honest, upright gentleman, but unsaved.

When his wife prayed for his salvation, he would laugh at her and tell her, "You had better be praying for some of these sinners. I'm all right." He gave money to the church to which his wife belonged. He gave money to the poor. He was doing a lot of good things as he went along the road of life, all the while neglecting the main thing.

His wife kept on praying for his salvation.

One night Daniel Currie said:

Along in the wee hours of the night, I saw a vision of myself trying to climb up to Heaven. I was making the ladder with my good works. Every time I gave some money to the church or helped a poor struggler along, I would place another rung in the ladder and climb a little higher. I would do something else good and climb a little higher still. It seemed that just one more rung in the ladder was all I needed.

There was the ledge of the Holy City; so when I gave some more money to the church, the rung slipped into place. I climbed up, took hold of the ledge, and pulled myself up. I said, "Who said I could not do it? Well here I am. I've made it." When I straightened up, there was a Man facing me, and on His head was a crown of thorns. His arms were outstretched in the shape of a cross. I saw the nailprints in His hands and heard Him say, "Daniel Currie, I am the door of the sheepfold. He that climbeth up any other way is a thief and a robber."

I awoke with a start. The dream was so real that I knew God was speaking to me. I woke my wife and said, "Sweetheart, get out of bed and pray for me." She said, "Pray for you? You have been telling me all these years that I had better pray for someone who was lost. What's the matter?" I said, "I know I am lost. I've been joking all the time. I am a lost man!"

That night, Daniel Currie and his wife knelt down in prayer, and the moral man received Jesus Christ as his Saviour and became a child of God.

Christ is the door. No man can get in any other way. To try to do so means to be cast out. Christ died on the cross for sinners. If you are still a sinner, come to Him now.

• • • •

SEEK THE SAVIOUR,
NOT A FEELING

In a revival meeting in Florida, a lady who regularly attended the church indicated that she wanted to be saved, but she didn't respond to the invitations. On her face was a look of sadness and anxiety, indicating inner confusion and perplexity. She listened to the preacher night after night, but she did not come forward.

One evening the evangelist hastened to meet her before she could get away. He asked if she would remain for a few moments and let him talk with her. She was glad to do so.

At first she seemed reluctant to disclose the barrier. The evangelist listed a number of things that might be hindering her from coming to the Saviour. He thought it might be a family hindrance or something in her past. Perhaps there was something that she did not want to give up. Perhaps she did not understand the Saviour's terms on which a lost sinner could find salvation in Him.

To the last question, she said, "Yes, that is it."

The evangelist said, "Open your heart and tell me how you feel."

She began to unburden her soul. "I have not been able to feel myself saved, and I am waiting for that feeling. I want to know I am saved; and how can I know it until a feeling comes? There is something I must do, and I don't know what it is. I have tried to be good and win Jesus' love, but the feeling doesn't come."

The evangelist said, "We have to be saved God's way, not ours. Let's see what the Bible says about salvation."

He gave the message of repentance, of faith. He quoted some Scriptures that tell us that man must repent, believing in Jesus Christ for salvation.

She came back with, "Yes, but I don't feel saved. One should have an experience upon which to base his hopes."

The evangelist said, "Is it not true that you have been seeking an experience, one that you have fashioned in your mind—an ecstatic feeling, overpowering joy, strange sights and sounds—when all the while you should have been seeking Jesus? To believe and know Him is an experience in itself."

Her face lighted up at once. "Oh, I see it! I see it! I thought there was something I had to do to save myself, when actually Jesus has already done it all for me."

This woman had been seeking a feeling instead of seeking the Saviour.

If you are going to be saved, it must be God's way, which is by a personal faith in Jesus Christ.

••••

THE POOR RICH MAN

A rich man went to New York and lived in a luxurious hotel. He watched the richly dressed people come and go. He listened to the muted music of a ballroom orchestra. He was seeing the kind of people and soaking up the kind of atmosphere he was used to.

Realizing how empty and futile his life had been, he decided to go down to the slums of New York and see how the people there lived, what kept them going, what motivated them day by day.

The next morning he found himself in a squalid section of the city. Standing in front of a little house, unpainted, weather-beaten and aged, he heard someone singing in the back of the house. When he turned the corner, he saw a woman doing the family washing. He stood and listened to her song; it was a song he had heard as a child. It took him back to the streets of memory. It reminded him of how far he had gone from God since he was a boy.

He asked the woman, "What makes you so happy in the midst of such poverty? I have had money and position and all that money can buy, but I don't have a heart for song."

She answered him, "Have a seat there on the steps. I will sit beside you and tell you of a great Friend who will keep me until the end."

When the rich man went back to the hotel, he was not

thinking about richly dressed people and the luxuries of life. He was thinking about just one thing—the Friend who would keep to the very end and throughout eternity.

Money cannot buy happiness nor a song in the heart. If you are like that "poor" rich man, I beseech you to seek what no amount of money can buy.

●●●●

DON'T COVER UP CHRIST!

I am reminded of the story of a pastor of a very old church in Richmond, Virginia. They were preparing for the celebration of the centennial. While he was doing some research, the pastor discovered that when the building was first erected, there was a large stained-glass window behind the pulpit and the choir. He wondered what had become of it.

Investigation revealed that the window, depicting Holman Hunt's "The Light of the World," was still in its original place. It wasn't seen because the outside had been bricked over by an adjoining building. Inside, massive organ pipes completely covered it.

Ah, my friend, is this not an illustration of the thing that is happening in too many of our churches, in too many of our homes, in too many of our lives? We have allowed artificial devices to cover up the picture of our Christ. We no longer hear His voice saying, "Behold, I stand at the door, and knock: if any man hear my voice, and open the door, I will come in to him, and will sup with him, and he with me."

Have an unveiling. Put Christ back in your life so others can see Him clearly.

> **Nothing between my soul and the Saviour,**
> **So that His blessed face may be seen;**
> **Nothing preventing the least of His favor,**
> **Keep the way clear! Let nothing between.**

●●●●

THE PERSONAL PRONOUN

Martin Luther is reported to have said, "The heart of religion is its personal pronoun."

Could he have been thinking of the 23rd Psalm, "The Lord is my shepherd"? or of Psalm 18:2 which abounds with personal pronouns: "The Lord is **my** rock, and **my** fortress, and **my** deliverer; **my** God, **my** strength, in whom **I** will trust; **my** buckler, and the horn of **my** salvation, and **my** high tower"?

We have all in Him—salvation, peace, power and assurance.

••••

"DADDY, I LOVED YOU EVEN IF YOU DID GET DRUNK"

Dr. George W. Truett, then pastor of First Baptist Church, Dallas, told a wonderful story about a father and son.

The little boy was accidentally shot one day by his neighbor-friend. Dr. Truett, the pastor, went to the home. He found doctors attending the child and heard them say, "He cannot live. The wound will kill him."

The boy did live for a time. Dr. Truett went back to see him. The first time he went, the father was there and was drinking. The next time he went, he was sobering up and in great agony of soul because of the suffering boy.

The pastor said he sat down beside the boy and tried to talk to him. The father knelt down, stroked the little boy's face, kissed him with all the affection of a mother, and said, "My little man is better, and he will soon be well."

The little boy said a strange thing: "No, Daddy, I will not get well."

The father protested, "Oh yes, you will soon be well, and I will be a good man. I will change my ways."

"When I am gone, Daddy, I want you to remember that I loved you even if you did get drunk."

That sentence broke the father's heart. He left the room, unable to tarry any longer. Dr. Truett later found him in the back of the cottage sobbing with a broken heart. Truett got down beside him and tried to comfort him, but the father said, "After my child loves me like that, oughtn't I straighten up and be the right kind of a man?"

Truett said, "I have a story ten thousand times sweeter than that to tell you." Then he told him the story of Jesus, how God sent His only Son to die on the cross that sinners might be saved. Dr. Truett made the story just as plain as possible. The big man then and there accepted Jesus Christ as his personal Saviour.

Dr. Truett said you could come into First Baptist Church on almost any Wednesday night; and if they were having testimonies, you would see this big man stand and hear him testify that the love of his boy brought him to Jesus. He would always relate his son's words, "Daddy, I loved you even if you did get drunk." He would testify that those words had turned him to Jesus, who loves the worst of sinners and died that men like him could be saved.

●●●●

THE CURE FOR BLINDNESS

Rose Crawford had been blind for fifty years. One day, after recovery from delicate surgery in an Ontario hospital, the doctor lifted the bandages from her eyes.

"I just can't believe it!" she cried. She wept for joy when for the first time in her life a dazzling and wonderful world of form and color greeted eyes that were now able to see.

The amazing thing about the story, however, is that twenty years of her blindness had been unnecessary. She didn't know that surgical techniques had been developed and that an operation could have restored her vision at the age of thirty. The doctor said, "She just figured that there was nothing that could be done about her condition. Much of her life could have been different."

Think of the millions of blinded people—blind to the Gospel. To them we must take the message of redeeming love. They must hear of Christ and of His power to save to the uttermost. Only Christ can cure spiritual blindness!

••••

COWPER'S CONVERSION

The story of William Cowper is very interesting. Though he was born in a preacher's family in 1731, he was not saved until he was in his thirties. He had a very sensitive spirit.

One day, turning to Romans 3:25, he read, "Whom God hath set forth to be a propitiation through faith in his blood, to declare his righteousness for the remission of sins that are past, through the forbearance of God."

When Cowper saw that it was Christ who bore his sins in His own body on the cross, he was then and there born into the family of God.

Cowper became a close friend of John Newton, the man who wrote "Amazing Grace."

Cowper wrote a poem entitled "Praise for the Fountain Opened." That's the song we sing which says:

> **There is a fountain filled with blood**
> **Drawn from Immanuel's veins;**
> **And sinners, plunged beneath that flood,**
> **Lose all their guilty stains.**
>
> **The dying thief rejoiced to see**
> **That fountain in his day;**
> **And there may I, though vile as he,**
> **Wash all my sins away.**

••••

FORTY-TWO YEARS LEARNING THREE LESSONS

An old man got up in one of D. L. Moody's meetings and said, "I have been forty-two years learning three things."

Said the great evangelist, "I pricked up my ears at that! I thought that if I could find out in three minutes what a man had taken forty-two years to learn, I should like to do it."

The first thing he said he learned was he could do nothing toward his own salvation. *Well,* Mr. Moody said to himself, *that is worth learning.*

The second thing he found out was God did not require him to do anything. *Well, that was worth learning,* Mr. Moody thought.

The third thing was that the Lord Jesus Christ had done it all, that salvation was finished, and that all he had to do was take it.

Mr. Moody said, "Dear friends, let us learn these same lessons."

••••

EIGHTEEN INCHES CAN MAKE AN ETERNAL DIFFERENCE

A few days ago someone sent me a gospel tract, "Missing Heaven by Eighteen Inches." The title was so unusual that I had to read the message. It simply stated that there is a big difference between the head and the heart. The distance is eighteen inches. A head knowledge of the Lord Jesus Christ will not save; there must be a heart acceptance of the Saviour.

"That if thou shalt confess with thy mouth the Lord Jesus, and shalt believe in thine heart that God hath raised him from the dead, thou shalt be saved.

"For with the heart man believeth unto righteousness; and with the mouth confession is made unto salvation."—Rom. 10:9, 10.

The tract closed with these words: "Eighteen inches can mean an eternity with Christ or an eternity without Christ."

Are you sure of your personal relationship to Him? Is it a head knowledge or a heart knowledge? Be sure you know the difference.

• • • •

VERY SICK, BUT VERY SAVED

Dr. Vance, a pastor in Nashville, Tennessee, for many years called on a Scotchman dying of tuberculosis. This is the story:

> Climbing up filthy, creaking stairs to a hall bedroom on the second floor, I entered a room in which I felt I could almost cut tubercular germs with a knife. It was in a most unsanitary condition. On the cot lay a man with an awful cough, with sunken cheeks and hollow eyes, in the last stages of consumption. He told me that he had run away from home when a boy and that, although his own parents in Scotland had been pious people, he had lived a wild and reckless life.
>
> He said he wanted me to help him get home. Supposing that he wanted to go back home to Scotland, I asked him if he was a member of the Saint Andrew's Society and how much money he would need.
>
> He told me that I did not understand him—that what he wanted was for me to show him how to get saved. Then I realized that the home he was talking about was the eternal Home.
>
> What could I say to this man? Could I talk to this dying man about his wicked life? Should I talk about Jesus Christ as an example? Should I expound to him the ethics of Jesus? Ah no! I told him the story of the Saviour who died for sinners.
>
> I watched that poor old soul turn to the Son of God and receive Him as Saviour. I saw the peace of God come into his heart and express itself on his face.

Here is the miracle of salvation which we have through our blessed Lord.

••••

LINCOLN INVITES AN OLD MAN TO SHARE HIS PEW

There is a beautiful story told about Abraham Lincoln worshiping in one of the Washington churches.

An old man slowly walked up the aisle, looking vainly for a seat. He was obviously embarrassed by his failure to find what he sought. Still unsuccessful, he started back toward the door. As he passed Lincoln's pew, the long arm of the president reached out to him, and his warm but rough voice whispered, "Come in here with me."

I like that story! Would it be wrong for me to say today that we are wandering up and down the lonely aisles of life; but we can hear the voice of our Saviour saying, "Come unto me...and I will give you rest"?

There is always room for one more. Christ never sends anyone away. His door is always open wide to receive mankind.

••••

WHO'S WHO IN AMERICA VERSUS THE LAMB'S BOOK OF LIFE

In our nation we have published the book entitled *Who's Who in America*. This book is a catalog of the so-called famous people of our nation. There have been about sixty-three thousand thumbnail biographies in it. They are now planning to expand it to include thirty thousand new names.

Names are in *Who's Who in America* because of some accomplishment, some significant achievement attained. It may be political work, social work or religious work.

It is altogether different in God's book. Your name is put

into the Lamb's book of life when you recognize yourself as a lost sinner and put your trust in the finished work of Jesus Christ.

• • • •

"I BELONG TO YOU!"

Charles Wellborn was in Italy during World War II, driving through the country with some of his friends. They came to a little town devastated by artillery. On the porch of a home sat a little boy, crying bitterly.

> We stopped, and the boy told us his story, then took us to the rear of the house. There in the ruined kitchen, he showed us the bodies of his father, mother and sister. He was alone in the world. We put him in a jeep and made him the mascot of our company.
>
> Little Tony, nine years old, won a place in our hearts. I managed to get some uniforms cut out to his size and a little cap to cock over one eye. On those rare occasions overseas when we stood review, Little Tony would be in the rear rank, as proud and straight as any soldier.
>
> Then one day the order came down that all waifs and refugees must be turned over to a central authority. Little Tony had to go, and I had to tell him. I didn't know how, except to remind him that he was a good soldier and good soldiers always obey orders. That night we stood review. This time, Tony stood beside the captain himself, receiving the parting salutes of his buddies.
>
> As the evening sun sank below the mountains and the silver notes of the bugle died away, Tony turned and marched toward the waiting jeep. About halfway there, Tony the soldier became Tony the little boy. With the tears streaming down his face, he came running back to throw his arms around my knees, to look up into my face, and say, "Don't you see? I can't go. I belong to you!"

Charles Wellborn closed that story by saying: "How many of us today need to throw our arms around the knees of God and say, 'I can't go away. I can't go away. I belong to You!'"

SECOND COMING

WORK AND LOOK WHILE WAITING

One night after I had preached in Jacksonville, Florida, I arranged for a man to pick me up at 3:30 the next morning so I could catch my plane at 4:50 to go home.

I went to my motel, got an alarm clock from the office, and set it for 3:15. I went to bed around midnight and thought I would go right to sleep, but I kept thinking about the alarm clock and about the time it would go off. I looked at it at 1:00 a.m. and then at 2:00 a.m. I glanced at it again at 3:00 a.m. I began wondering how the alarm would sound when it went off. Would it be loud or soft? Would it awaken me if I went to sleep? I think the time from 3:00 to 3:15 was the longest I have ever known.

At 3:10 a.m. I got up on the edge of the bed and looked at the clock. I waited for it to go off at 3:15. When it finally started to ring, it seemed to explode like a shotgun! Relieved, I turned it off. I could get up now and begin traveling.

I offer this simple illustration to say that it is far better that we don't know the time of the coming of our Lord. We can work through the day rejoicing as we work and look expectantly toward His return. We can lie down to sleep at night when troubled, resting in the Lord and knowing that in His hands all things will be done right.

"And to wait for his Son from heaven, whom he raised from the dead, even Jesus, which delivered us from the wrath to come."— I Thess. 1:10.

• • • •

BE NEAR TO JESUS

It is said that when Captain Eddie Rickenbacker and his companions of the ill-fated air expedition in the South Seas prepared to abandon their plane, they threw out everything that was movable. "Staring at the face of Death!" Captain Rickenbacker has since said. "If you ever think that material things are worth anything, have that experience, and you will find out how useless they are, no matter how you may have cherished them."

Get rid of everything that would hinder you from looking for His return. You can take nothing with you; all material things must be left behind.

Get ready for the trumpet sound!

SERVICE

"COACH, I JUST HAD TO SUCCEED WITH MY DAD LOOKING ON!"

James Jeffrey, director of the Fellowship of Christian Athletes, tells his favorite story about Bill Carroway:

Bill, an athlete, never made the first string at Georgetown University. Time came for the last game of the season and the last football game of Bill's career—his last chance to play.

The night before the game he went to Coach Lou Little and asked if he could get in the game "for just one play." The coach promised that he would do his best to carry out his wishes.

At halftime Georgetown was three points behind, and Bill had never left the bench. During the second half, the Georgetown offense couldn't seem to get going. Bill put his helmet under his arm and began walking up and down the sidelines in front of the coach, hoping to be seen. The coach saw him and sent Bill into the game.

On the first play Bill took the handoff from the quarterback and ran forty yards downfield before being pulled out of bounds. The fans cheered and looked at their program. Bill's name was not on it.

Seconds remained in the game. On the next play the quarterback faded back to pass. Bill Carroway broke away from his defender. The pass came spiraling through the air. He caught it and fell into the end zone for the winning touchdown. Georgetown won the championship.

Coach Little sought out Bill in the dressing room and said, "I have never seen a boy more determined than you were today. What gave you this overwhelming desire to win this game?"

Bill looked at his coach and answered, "My mother died when I was born, and my father raised me. He wanted only two things of me—to get a college education and to play football. I knew my dad would never see me play football because he was blind, but a few days ago he died. I knew that today would be the first and last time he would ever have a chance to see his son play. Coach, I just had to succeed with my dad looking on!"

What a beautiful story! It should cheer all of us to go on to do greater things for our Saviour.

Our Saviour and a grandstand are watching our performance and cheering us on. Let's not disappoint any of them! Play the game of life well, then the Saviour will say, "Well done, Daughter," or "Well done, Son."

●●●●

"WHEN, IF NOT NOW?
WHO, IF NOT YOU?"

The life story of Jane Addams of Hull House on Chicago's West Side teaches, among other things, to do the job now.

Because of her social work with the poor and underprivileged, she won the Nobel Peace Prize. She made poor boys and girls rich in the character and tradition of our early fathers in the basic elements of good citizenship.

The secret of Miss Addams' benevolence and her passion for social justice lay in two questions, questions which were the driving force of her fruitful life: When, if not now? and, Who, if not you?

Take a lesson from this woman. When should we do the work of Christ? Now! Who should do the work of Christ? You! God has appointed you to this task. Do not fail to give out this unchanging message.

••••

MISTAKEN IDENTITY

Kilpin was once mistaken for John Bunyan on the streets of Bedford. A man accosted him, slapped him a fierce blow in the face, and said, "Take that, John Bunyan!"

Kilpin took off his hat and said, "I will take fifty times as much as that to have the honor to be called John Bunyan!"

What an honor to be a servant of our Lord! What an honor to suffer in His service!

••••

"THE LAZIEST MAN"

Some folks are almost as lazy as the man I read about who lived up in the mountains.

He won the title of "The Laziest Man." A gentleman from the sponsoring company came to deliver the one-thousand-dollar prize. When the door opened, he said, "Where is Mr. Jackson, the laziest man in the world?"

"He's down by the creek," was the reply.

He found him lying down, not moving a muscle, with his eyes closed. The bearer of the prize said, "I have your one-thousand-dollar prize, and I want to give it to you."

The mountaineer said, "Roll me over and put it in my left pocket."

There are some Christians who are just about that lazy. They never take a step to talk to their neighbors, never open their mouths to say a good word for Jesus, never turn a page in their Bibles to show a sinner how to be saved. In other words, they are lazy. If that hits you, I hope it hurts!

••••

JOHN WESLEY RESCUED!

When John Wesley was a child, there was a fire in his home. The family hurried away from the burning building. In the excitement the eighth child was forgotten. A neighbor climbed a short ladder and reached the child in time. That child was John Wesley.

There would never have been a Wesley revival if it had not been for the quick thinking of an unnamed neighbor. God used this person to rescue the child who became the famous evangelist.

There is a task for you to perform in this world. Jump at that opportunity for service. Rescue the perishing while you can; soon it may be too late.

• • • •

IS HE HANDICAPPED?

Pastor R. D. Wade of Austin, Texas, tells about a man named Robert Miller, who was born without arms or legs. He was converted and is now an evangelist. The pastor speaks highly of him.

Robert is a university graduate, drives his own car, writes his own letters, and sings the Gospel. He is an effective speaker. This man who came into the world "handicapped" is fearlessly giving out the Word of God.

Avail yourself of all opportunities for serving Christ. If Robert Miller can do it, so can you!

• • • •

"JUST SHOW HIM YOUR HANDS!"

As a humble Christian woman lay dying, she lamented to her pastor how little she had been able to do for Jesus. With no formal education, she worked in a factory, saving every penny she could to send to missions. It wasn't much, but she gave what she could. After work, she visited the sick, often doing their washing and ironing at night.

As she faced her final moments on earth, she explained, "Oh, I have been able to do so little for the Lord! I have never had much money to give, for all I could do was common labor."

Looking at her gnarled hands, deformed by hard work and arthritis, the pastor gently said, "Beloved, when you stand before the Lord, just show Him your hands."

That Christian woman had done what she could, and the Lord asks no more.

"And Jesus sat over against the treasury, and beheld how the people cast money into the treasury: and many that were rich cast in much.

"And there came a certain poor widow, and she threw in two mites, which make a farthing.

"And he [Jesus] called unto him his disciples, and saith unto them, Verily I say unto you, That this poor widow hath cast more in, than all they which have cast into the treasury:

"For all they did cast in of their abundance; but she of her want did cast in all that she had, even all her living."—Mark 12:41–44.

• • • •

SERVING WITHOUT SEEING

General Booth, founder of the Salvation Army, went blind in his latter years. He had been lying in bed for many weeks, and the doctor didn't know how to tell him he would never see again. finally the doctor told his son, Bramwell, that he would have to tell his father.

Bramwell went into the old general's room and said, "Dad, the doctor tells me that you'll never see again."

The old general's jaw muscles tightened, and he said, "Bramwell, do you mean I will never look into your face again?"

"Not this side of Heaven, Father," Bramwell replied.

Then across the counterpane came the gnarled old hand of the general and took hold of his son's hand. "Son, I have done the best I could to serve my God and my people with my eyes; now I'll do my best to serve my God and my people without my eyes."

What can you say against a man like that? Nothing! Such a man had great victory in his soul, and that victory was declared to the whole world.

God grant that a little bit of such determination would rub off on each of us. Let us make our choices about service—handicapped or not.

● ● ● ●

CRUSHING BRINGS PERFECTION

A distinguished musician ordered a violin manufacturer to make him the best instrument possible. "Use the best materials, take all the time necessary, and use all your skill in its construction."

Some months later the manufacturer sent for the musician to come try the violin. As the musician drew the bow across the strings, his face clouded with disappointment. Lifting the violin, he smashed it to pieces, paid for it, and left the shop.

The maker was not satisfied with this. "I will, with those fragments, construct a violin which is worthy of the artist's skill," he vowed.

He again sent for the musician. This time the frown was not there. The musician recognized the perfection of the work.

"What is the price?" he asked.

"Nothing," replied the manufacturer. "It is the same instrument you smashed to pieces."

Often crushing defeats and disappointments must be ours in order to make us into the instruments that God can use.

SIN

AARON BURR'S TRAGIC DECISION

At the age of nineteen, Aaron Burr was a brilliant student in Princeton University. When a revival broke out on the campus, his roommate urged him to accept Christ. Burr was almost persuaded.

He went to see one of his professors and told him of his dilemma. The professor gave him a Bible and said, "Go to your room and settle this matter on your knees." However, instead of doing this, he tried to shake off the conviction of the Holy Spirit.

Finally, in desperation, he cried out, "God, You let me alone, and I'll let You alone!" As soon as he said it, all conviction left him.

Years later he met a friend whom he admired very much.

"Burr," this friend said, "I would like for you to meet a Friend of mine."

"If he is anything like you, I will be happy to meet him."

"His name is Jesus Christ. I want you to meet Him."

The cold sweat popped out on Burr's forehead. Then he told about how, at the age of nineteen, he had said, "God, You let me alone, and I'll let You alone!" Then he added, "From that day to this, I have never had one desire to become a Christian."

I may not understand that full story, but this I do know: when a man turns his back upon the Lord Jesus Christ, there is nothing between him and Hell.

While the Holy Spirit pleads, open your heart's door and invite Him in. He will not always plead—as in the case of Aaron Burr. It is easy to turn to Christ and accept His gift to you.

••••

THE WORLD'S GREATEST VICE

Mr. Lee Bristol, president of the Bristol-Meyers Company of New York, wrote an article entitled "This I Believe."

In it he referred to the "greatest worldwide vice." In a day like this, I suppose many would begin thinking about what it might be. You might talk about gambling, drunkenness, prostitution, graft, lying, stealing, murder, suicide or war.

However, here is what Mr. Bristol said: "The world's greatest vice is *selfishness*."

It was selfishness that had a hold on the Pharisees; they put self ahead of God. They wanted to satisfy their own desires rather than to help people in need.

Someone said, "Turn the world's greatest vice—selfishness—into the world's greatest virtue—service—and you yourself will have happiness and bring happiness to others."

••••

THE TWO POSTERS

Many years ago in Kentucky, the communists put on an advertising campaign in some of the mining sections of the eastern part of the state. This was back in the day when *communism* was a relatively strange word. We did not know as much about it then as now.

There were two big posters used in various mining sections of the state. One had the picture of the torso of a man with a group of men standing around the torso, and with knives they were cutting into the torso. The picture showed them eating the body of the man. The atheistic Russians had put under this picture the words of Scripture, "Take, eat: this is my body."

The other poster sent into eastern Kentucky by the communists pictured a bartender sweeping out a saloon. In front of his big broom were broken bottles, cigar butts, dirt, filth and vomit. In the midst of all this was a statuette, and tied to it was a card. On the card was the name "God." On the bottom of the poster were these words, "This is what we are doing to your God in Russia."

As we look at the condition of nations today, we can well see that Satan is at work. In spite of the efforts of good men, there are still widespread wickedness and evil controlling the actions of nations.

•••

THE DEAD RAT

Hadley Page, the flyer, tells of a flight he was making in Arabia in one of the old-time planes.

A large rat got into the plane without his knowledge. When he got up in the air, he knew the rat was gnawing on a vital part of the plane. The rat's razor-sharp teeth might damage some parts that would cause a crash. What could he do?

Remembering that a rat cannot live in high altitude, he pulled his plane straight up into the heavens. After a time the gnawing stopped. When he returned to the ground, he found the rat was dead. It could not exist in the high atmosphere.

This lesson is good for us. Evil cannot exist in an atmosphere lived in dedication to Christ.

••••

SELFISHNESS BROUGHT DEATH

A man's love for money is partially illustrated by this story, given by an elderly lady in southern Illinois:

Many years ago when I was a young girl, a rabid dog in our rural community bit me and a young man. Serum for the treatment of rabies was not locally available back then. So, the dog's owner offered to pay our full expenses to Chicago for the inoculation or give us five hundred dollars in cash.

I boarded the Illinois Central train for Chicago and stayed the time necessary for adequate treatment.

In the 1890s, five hundred dollars looked like a fortune; so the young man said he would prefer the cash and assume the risk of not securing medical aid.

When I returned home, the unfortunate boy was dead and buried.

You may think this an extreme example of selfishness, but not so. There are people now driving themselves into premature graves because of the love of money. Ambition has seized their hearts, and they can see nothing else.

● ● ● ●

REVIVAL—OR REVOLUTION

I was in conference with an excellent minister of the Gospel in another state who was depressed and discouraged about his ministry. He had been pastor of a church for many months without any significant results. A few had been saved, but the general attitude of the people revealed the lack of any burden for the lost. The reason for his conference with me was as follows:

On the previous Sunday morning he had given an invitation for the unsaved to come and receive the Lord Jesus. A woman in the city came forward and said she wanted Christ as her Saviour. The pastor had the joy of leading her to the Lord.

After he had finished his spiritual dealing with this soul, he turned to the audience and asked for an expression of their joy in her salvation. He noticed a definite hesitation of the people to express themselves.

At the end of the service, one of his deacons came to him and said, "Pastor, it is all right for this woman to get saved— there is nothing we can do about this—but we do not want her in the church. She operates a dress shop downtown, but she is known far and wide for the sinfulness of her conduct; she is an immoral person." Others shared the same opinion as this deacon. The pastor was disturbed about the attitude of his people. The church had long been a proud, wealthy church. They had never entered into evangelism to reach the poor and downtrodden.

I did not know what advice to give this pastor. I simply suggested that he go back to his church and preach the Gospel to sinners. If sinners got saved he could rejoice, even if his people did not rejoice. I assured the pastor that I was sure God would give him either a revival or a revolution— maybe both.

•••••

THE GREAT PHYSICIAN—THE ANSWER TO DRUG ADDICTION

The drug habit got hold of a man. Everything that he had was sacrificed to his awful sin. He sought release from every source known to him.

Then he went to an old physician who believed in the power of God. The suffering man said, "Doctor, I have only fifty dollars left in the world. I will gladly give it to you and more—if I can—if you will save me and my family from the ruin that awaits us."

The doctor wisely answered, "There is no hope for you in yourself. Only the Great Physician can be of service to you. Today He will save you if you will come to Him in repentance."

That sinner, addicted to the drug habit, went away, but he couldn't get away from the words of the doctor and the Bible which had been read to him.

One night he fell upon his face, threw away his drugs, and cried to God for salvation. God saved him, and at once he began to live a life of victory.

SORROW

SWEETEST LESSONS LEARNED
ON THE ROAD OF SORROW

The grandstands teach us so little! It may be enjoyable to sit in the grandstand and watch the game, but the lessons are few. No one ever became a great football player by sitting in the grandstand, nor did any person ever become a great baseball pitcher or a home-run hitter like Babe Ruth by sitting in the stands and clapping his hands. We have to come away from the grandstand and participate.

We learn so little by looking on pleasurable events, but we learn much in sorrow. Sorrow, like suffering, brings us into the arena of life. Quite often I have had experience with those who have tried to avoid the road of sorrow.

In recent years I have had more and more people tell me at a funeral of a loved one that they did not want any songs nor any tears; and quite often they have wanted just as brief a message as possible. They were trying to avoid the road of sorrow.

This is very foolish, for some of the sweetest lessons of life can come upon this road. Sorrow quite often can bring us down from the grandstand onto the road of life. Sorrow brings us in touch with reality. Sorrow gives us sympathy for others.

You can look at a man having difficulties as long as you care to, but you will never understand his trouble until you yourself have the same trouble. We cannot sit in the grandstand, look upon those who are blindly stumbling along the tragic road of sorrow, and understand their problems. We must come down.

First, don't fear sorrow. Some are always fearful that some sorrow will come their way, so they try to protect themselves. Don't fear sorrow! You have One who will be with you through every heartache of life. The Saviour gave these words for you and for me:

"Let not your heart be troubled: ye believe in God, believe also in me.

"In my Father's house are many mansions: if it were not so, I would have told you. I go to prepare a place for you."—John 14:1,2.

Second, don't ignore sorrow. Let your sorrows teach you the pointed lessons of life. Let your sorrows open your eyes so you can understand the heartaches, the afflictions and the needs of others.

Third, don't try to cover your sorrows. Death took away a very fine, sweet wife from a man's side. His heart was broken, and everyone knew it. A few hours after the funeral service, he tried to cover his sorrow by getting drunk. This is foolish. Face the sorrows of life! Come down from the grandstand onto the highway and learn to live victoriously with your sorrows.

Some are prone to shut themselves off from others when there is sorrow. They refuse to learn lessons from God, and they refuse to take His sustenance and comfort.

Come, my friends, to the Lord. Bring every sorrow to Him. He walks in the main pathway of life. He understands your need and will give you the comfort needed. His help is available. Come and take it.

SOUL WINNING

MODERN NOAH

I saw a most amazing story on the front page of a newspaper. It read "Modern Noah Halted."

The story was out of Santa Ana, California. It told about the police's hearing strange noises coming from a thirty-five-foot house trailer where Johnny Riverfoot and his wife lived. Inside the trailer were three 150-pound bears, a burro, a wallaby, an ocelot, a bobcat, three goats, two opossums, three peacocks, thirteen dogs, four cats, six pigeons, five doves, three rabbits, five guinea pigs, nine chickens, two geese, sixteen quail, two desert turtles and a duck! The newspaper said, "All appeared healthy."

Mr. Riverfoot said he was a circus and carnival clown and he used all of the animals in his act. The newspaper said it took six truckloads to carry the menagerie to the Orange County animal shelter!

The picture is extreme, I know; but sometimes our churches get so involved with a multitude of things that they fail to do the major thing—winning souls.

SUFFERING

AN IMAGINARY SCENE

Mark 2:1–12 is a story known to all of us—a story of suffering and of the healing power of our Saviour. Someone suggested this interesting imaginary epilogue to the story:

> The day after Jesus had healed the crowds in the low-ceiling house, a man came briskly down the street looking for a house. His step was elastic, and his whole appearance suggested the vigor and eagerness of youth. He paused before a door and looked in. On a scaffold, precariously poised, a lone workman was plastering the ceiling. The floor and the doorway were cluttered with debris.
>
> The young man greeted the plasterer, "Good morning, neighbor. What are you doing?"
>
> There was a slight delay. The workman looked toward the doorway before pleasantly answering, "Oh, have you not heard about the excitement here yesterday? There was a young man here, a Healer from Galilee. The place was jammed with people who came to be cured, and He used this house for His ministry. Scribes were here too, and they didn't seem to like some of the things He said; but the big excitement was when four fellows brought a poor palsied wretch and, being unable to crowd into the room, tore open this roof here and lowered the sick man right down in front of the Healer. He seemed pleased by it and cured the paralytic and commended his friends."
>
> "Yes," observed the young man with an inflection that indicated amusement.

"Who may you be, if I may ask," went on the workman; "and how happens it that you have not heard this strange story?"

There was a pause before the answer came: "I'm the palsied wretch," he said smiling.

"Indeed! And how do you feel?"

"Why, I feel great! By the way, whose house is this? I thought I would come around and offer to repair the damage my friends caused."

The workman laughed, carefully descended from the scaffolding, straightened himself up, and proudly answered, "I'm the owner, and you owe me nothing. As a matter of fact, I've been thinking for some time that my roof was in pretty bad shape and needed attention. I have a new one now, and we are all much better off, it seems; but I confess, I never thought it would come about in such a way as this!"

• • • •

SUFFERING BRINGS COMPASSION

A little lady was on a bus going to New Orleans. She was timid and afraid.

The bus stopped, and a new passenger got on. She sat down beside the timid lady and said, "Where are you going?"

"My doctor is sending me to Charity Hospital in New Orleans. I have cataracts," she answered.

The newcomer said, "I am also on my way to New Orleans. Don't worry; I will help you."

The two got off the bus together. The stronger woman led her new friend to the admitting office of the hospital and remained with her until she was admitted and assigned to a ward. She came back again and again to see her. When her timid friend was dismissed from the hospital to go home, she was there.

"I will have to come back in a few days for an examination by my doctor."

"I will find you a place to stay."

This went on for some time. Finally, the timid lady said to her good friend, "I can't thank you enough. You have been so good to me. Tell me, why have you done all of this?"

The Samaritan lady said quietly, but with deep feeling, "I have been sick too."

"I am so sorry. You are well now, aren't you?"

"Yes, thank the Lord, and thanks to the doctors at Charity Hospital too." Then she said, "You know, the doctor said I was in danger of going blind. I too had cataracts."

The illustration is a clear one. Our sufferings will enable us to have more sympathy for others. Our sufferings will keep us away from the nonessentials. Our sufferings will draw us near to the Saviour.

• • • •

THE SCHOOL OF ADVERSITY

Life without adversity and suffering would be pretty much like life without character. It was Newell Dwight Hillis who said:

> No Phidias ever polished his marble with softness and warmth. Perfection is through the chisel and sharp blows of the mallet. Steel is iron plus fire, tools are wood plus gashing axes, and statues are marble plus the chisel whose every stroke makes the sparks to fly.

The Lord Jesus may allow you to be sick or to remain sick or weak of body in order to use you in a greater way. I do not say that I can explain this, but I know it is true. History is full of noteworthy examples of individuals who had great handicaps and yet were mightily used to do extraordinary works.

Milton, the poet, was blind; Beethoven, the musician, was deaf.

From his blindness, Milton could write *Paradise Lost*. From his deafness, Beethoven could write the *Eighth Symphony*. From the Bedford jail, Bunyan could write *Pilgrim's Progress*.

It is said that Francis Parkman could not work longer than five minutes at a time—so great was his pain; and so weak were his eyes, he had to scrawl a few huge words on a piece of paper. Yet Francis Parkman gave to the world twenty magnificent volumes of history.

Pasteur was paralyzed. In his laboratory he bent over his animals and test tubes. How much does this world owe to Pasteur who worked so sacrificially!

Sir Henry Fawcett, when a young man, lost the sight of both eyes through an accidental shooting by his father. So anxious was he to comfort his father that he made great efforts to accomplish more than he might have with his sight. He became a college professor, a member of Parliament, and postmaster general of England.

Down in Alabama you can go by the spot where Helen Keller was born. She was blind, deaf and mute. In spite of these handicaps, she learned to do all that we can do and much more.

I repeat that some sickness or weakness of body may be allowed to remain upon you in order that our Saviour might use you in a greater way.

SURRENDER

WHEN JOHN WESLEY SURRENDERED

For more than thirty years John Wesley was a failure. He had a good education and plenty of opportunities for service, but he was not surrendered completely to the will of God. He was not filled with the Holy Spirit. It was when he came to that place of total surrender in his ministry that his name became known around the world.

Note also, when John Wesley was fully surrendered to the Lord, he said, "Your business is not to preach so many sermons and to take care or this or that society, but to win as many souls as you can."

••••

FULLY SURRENDERED

The year was 1872. The setting was a small congregation gathered in a barn for a gospel service. A quiet-spoken preacher by the name of Henry Varley was concluding a message on I John 2:17. Lifting his eyes to the nearby haymow where an interested youth was seated, he said with emphasis, "The world has yet to see what God can do with, for, in, and through one man who is fully consecrated to Him!"

The intent listener was strangely stirred and convicted by those challenging words.

Varley meant any man, he said to himself. *He didn't say he had to be educated or brilliant or anything else—just a person willing to be used! Well, by the Holy Spirit in me, I will try to be such a man!*

Within a few years, the whole world had felt the impact of the life of that earnest young fellow who surrendered himself to the will of God on the day that Henry Varley preached. He became the great evangelist Dwight L. Moody.

He recognized that if God's will was to be done through him, self-will must die. He had to turn his back on the things of the world—"the lust of the flesh, and the lust of the eyes, and the pride of life"—and let the Holy Spirit take full control of his every thought and action.

•••

A STORY OF SUCCESS, THEN FAILURE, THEN GREATER SUCCESS

Nat Campbell lived in Louisville, Kentucky. He attended the church where I worked for two years. He was wealthy and came to church each Sunday morning in a limousine driven by a chauffeur.

His mother was always with him. He brought her into the church and sat near the rear of the building. At the first opportunity after service he would escort her out the door, put her in the car, and then drive away. We always knew when Mr. Campbell was present, for in the collection plate would be a one-hundred-dollar bill. (A hundred dollars was a tremendous sum of money back in the depression days.)

I was called to a church in Memphis, Tennessee. After being gone from Louisville for some time, I returned for a visit and attended my old church. They were having a choir party. A group of singers were meeting in one of the Sunday school rooms. The pastor was also present.

He led me into the room and introduced me to a man. He said, "I want you to meet Mr. Campbell."

"Yes, I know Mr. Campbell. I used to see him come into

the church when I was here some time ago."

"But this is a different Mr. Campbell," said the pastor.

I looked at him, and he surely seemed to be different. There was a smile on his face. The suit he had on was not extravagant.

Then Mr. Campbell began to speak: "When you were here, I would come to church, bring my mother, sit on the back seat, and rush out of the building as soon as I could. After you left, I lost everything. The depression wiped out my business. I am now working for wages."

Then with a big smile on his face, Mr. Campbell said, "But I am the happiest man in this city! When my success in financial matters was taken away, God brought me back to Himself. I had been saved for many years, but I had been far away from God. When I lost everything, it brought me back into submission to Him."

Then the pastor spoke up: "Yes, Mr. Campbell is now teaching the men's Bible class of our church and is one of our most active members."

I would say that this is a story of success, then failure, then a greater success—success in the things of God!

TESTIMONY

A CHRISTIAN SHOULD ACT
LIKE A CHRISTIAN

A Christian man had his office in a downtown building. One day there came a frantic knocking on his inner office door. He rushed out of his office to find that anxious friends had placed a hysterical woman on the divan and were doing all in their power to quiet her.

Hurriedly, they told the businessman that the woman had come to the doctor's office next door with her husband, who was to have minor surgery. When the anesthetic was administered, there had been a terrible reaction, and the man had suddenly died.

It was his wife who lay screaming and twitching on the divan. Going over to her, the Christian businessman murmured soft words of condolence. He leaned over, put his face close to her distorted one, then asked, "Madam, are you a Christian?"

Like a dash of cold water, the shock hit her. Opening her eyes, she looked at him and replied, "Yes, I am."

Then he said, "Well, be one right now!"

What he said hit her like a bolt from the blue and awakened her conscience to what she was and had.

She arose from the divan, went back to the doctor's office, and began giving directions for the removal and care of her husband's body.

She gave a beautiful testimony to the sustaining power of

the Christ who is triumphant over death.

••••

HOW A PROFESSOR INFLUENCED A STUDENT

A disheveled student at Columbia University came into a morning church service in New York City. He crept into a back seat and sat down.

He had spent the night wandering through the streets of the city, battling with his doubts; now he was seeking a haven of rest. He was wondering if anything could give a man peace and satisfaction.

That morning he looked over the audience and saw one of his professors, a great scientist and a good teacher at Columbia. Having had him for a class, this young man knew something of the high position of this man in the academic world; yet he saw the big man sitting there with head bowed in prayer and listening to the sermon.

The young man thought, *If a man like that can believe in God and Jesus Christ, I can too.*

He walked out of the building a believer. He had heard the message of Christ from the pulpit, but he saw the work of Christ in the life of a man he respected. The professor knew nothing of what happened that Sunday morning.

One day a medical missionary returned to this country. This man's name was heralded in the newspaper as being one of the greatest contributors to medical missions that the nation has had for a quarter of a century. The first person he went to see when he got to New York City was his professor, now retired. Sitting in the professor's study, he told him of that Sunday morning when Christ spoke to his heart as a result of seeing him in the service.

••••

WHAT TEN CENTS DID
FOR A BUS DRIVER

A preacher got on a city bus, gave the driver a dollar, and received change in silver. He walked to the back of the bus. He saw that the driver had given him ten cents too much. Knowing that the money was not his, he walked back and handed the driver the dime saying, "You gave me too much change."

The driver replied, "Yes, I know I did. I watched you in the mirror when you saw that I had overpaid you. You do not know me, but I know you are a preacher. I was just trying a little experiment. If you had kept that dime, I would not have had confidence in preachers."

Whether the attitude of the bus driver is right or wrong is not pertinent to our story. We must be conscious that people are watching us. We must live so others will not be disappointed in us.

••••

"NO MAN WOULD HAVE BEEN HEROIC
THEN WHO IS NOT HEROIC NOW!"

In the late twilight of his life, Wendell Phillips, the great foe and fighter of slavery, sat by the fire one night talking to a young friend. The veteran abolitionist completely lost himself in a thrilling recital of the heroic days of long ago. The youth sat enthralled.

Finally, under the spell of the memorable evening, he rose to leave. "Mr. Phillips," he said as he took the old man's hand, "had I lived in your time, I think I would have been heroic too!"

That remark aroused the ire of the veteran who had accompanied the young visitor to the door. Pointing down the street, he drew the attention of his companion to the glaring indications of entrenched evil. Then in a voice trembling with indignation, he exclaimed, "Young man, you are living in *my* time and in *God's* time. Be sure of this: no man would have been heroic then who is not heroic now! Good night!"

There is always a danger that we will think it was easy for someone else. We sit in this twentieth century and imagine that it might have been simple to have testified for Christ in the first century—but not so—it has ever been the same. Every age has seen man fighting Satan, the world and the flesh. There is no difference.

WEDDINGS

MY WORLD-FAMOUS WEDDING STORY

I never thought I would put this story in print. I have told it in churches in every part of the United States and Canada. (This is my story! Some other preachers have sought to tell it as though it happened to them, but not so—this is mine!)

I was pastor at a church in Tennessee when I received a call from my friend Elbert Gallagher, asking me to be the best man at his wedding. The wedding was scheduled to take place in Louisville at the Virginia Avenue Baptist Church. I told Elbert I could be there for the wedding but I could not be there for the rehearsal. He agreed that it would be all right to miss the rehearsal since I would have no part except to walk by his side in the wedding ceremony.

I drove to Louisville on a Friday (I don't recall the exact date) and arrived a few minutes before 8:00 p.m.—the time of the wedding. I went to the room just back of the pulpit and found the pastor, Brother Benedict, pacing the floor. When I asked what was wrong, he said that the groom had not arrived and it was time for the wedding music to begin.

Perhaps I had better pause here to say a few words about my good friend Elbert Gallagher. Through the years I have met many thousands of people, but Elbert still remains one of the most unusual men I have ever met.

He was a fine musician and could sing and play the piano beautifully. He was a star magician. I have watched him

mystify hundreds of people with feats of magic. He was a
strong man—not a large man, but strong, with mighty
power in his hands and arms. I have watched him crush
bricks and blocks of concrete with his bare knuckles.

One day we stood before the big oak door in a house in
Louisville, and Elbert asked, "Do you want to see me break
that door with one blow?"

When I said, "Yes," he pulled back his arm and struck the
door with his fist. The door was cracked from top to bottom.

Elbert had a photographic memory. He could memorize
chapters in the Bible with one reading. He could memorize
and preach a sermon by Dr. R. G. Lee with just a reading. At
one time I heard him quote a magnificent poem—twenty-
five minutes in length—never missing a word!

Back to the story...he was late for his own wedding!

Brother Benedict told the singers to present their songs,
confident that Elbert would arrive any moment. The songs
were finished by 8:20, and still no bridegroom.

The organist played until about 8:30, then she stopped!
The distressed pastor was pacing the floor. This had never
happened before in his ministry. The bride was at the door
of the church holding the arm of her father. All the atten-
dants were ready, but the wedding could not begin—
no bridegroom!

Suddenly the pastor turned to me. "Brother Roberson,
you were the singer in the church for two years; go out
and sing for them. This will keep the crowd quiet until
Elbert arrives."

I quickly answered, "No sir, I can't. I don't know any wedding songs except 'I Love You Truly' and 'Because,' and the
singers have already used them."

He paced a little more. Then he turned and said, "Go out
and sing a hymn or a gospel song. Just anything will help at
this time."

I said, "Pastor, I have never done anything like this, but I will do my best."

I left his study and climbed the steps to the choir loft. As I entered the choir loft I picked up a hymnbook, opened it, turned a few pages, stepped over to the organ, and told the organist I would sing number 416.

She turned to the number and began playing an introduction.

I walked to the platform of the church. With songbook in hand, I stood back of the pulpit. Flowers were everywhere—roses, lilies, violets. The pulpit stand was engulfed with flowers. I stood back of the stand and put my face between the roses and the lilies. The audience looked at me and made no response.

The songbook was in my hand. I prepared to sing. (Perhaps I should say that in the early days of my singing I had a voice of tremendous volume. I needed no public address system.) Now I was ready. The organ played, and I began to sing. (It was now 8:40 p.m.) I sang with all the force of my being. Do you know what I had picked out? "I Come to the Garden Alone"!

I sang one line, and the audience roared. They laughed and clapped their hands. I saw what I had done, so I got down as low as I could and slunk back to the pastor's study.

Brother Benedict looked at me with great pity and said, "Son, I think that was a mistake!" (His was the understatement of the year!)

I told this story a few years ago in Denver, Colorado. Because of a delayed arrival by plane, I was late for the service. I thought I would ease the tension—so I told the wedding story and went on with my sermon. I finished my message and stood at the front of the church shaking hands with some people. I looked up and saw two dear old ladies coming down the aisle toward me, serious and shaking. As they walked up to me, one put her finger right up in my face and said, "We heard your story, Preacher. We want to know just one thing: did he ever get there?"

Yes, he got there an hour late. I walked in with Elbert, but I did not feel like a "best man."

WITNESSING

A GREAT WORK DONE
BY A HANDICAP

Paul Rader, an evangelist, told the story about a dear saint of God who lived in a grove. He owned a bubbling spring of water bordering the roadside. The old saint knew his Lord and walked with Him daily. He was crippled and misshapen and unfit for any earthly toil requiring physical strength, so he sat the weary days through in his home in the grove.

Years passed, but he still had a great desire to do something to help others. Bitter tears of disappointment streamed down his face as the awful realization of his weak physical condition swept over him. He struggled in prayer. He felt he would die if he could not go and tell others of Christ.

Then in a lovely night of prayer, the Spirit lifted the load and said, "Stay! Stay by the road! There are many sinners there!"

The old saint of God had the spring dug out by the side of the road and, with rock selected from the brook, built up walls around the side and hung a dipper to a chain. Behind the spring, he had a rustic seat circling temptingly. Then he spent a little more of his small allowance to hire a carpenter to move his little house closer to the spring. With his own hands, he was able to plant flowers and trim the shrubs.

Daily the old man sat on the rustic seat and greeted the

passersby. When they stopped to get a drink of cold water, he engaged them in conversation. He offered them a seat in the shade and then would tell them the story of Jesus Christ.

Day after day, he went on with this ministry until literally hundreds and thousands had heard the Gospel through the lips of the old man sitting by the spring at the side of the road.

Yes, the handicapped can have a great ministry "beside the road" or on his bed of affliction.

• • • •

A LIVING SACRIFICE

A Moravian missionary to the West Indies found he could not get to the natives. He yearned to reach them for Christ, but they worked throughout the day and were too tired at night and too exhausted to listen to his preaching. He tried many things to get them under the sound of the Gospel, but all without success.

After everything had failed, he thought of Romans 12:1 and decided to make a drastic move. He sold himself as a slave to one of the plantation owners and was driven with the colored men into the field to work. Here at odd moments he had the opportunity to talk to the natives. It is said that, though he "lost his life" for the Gospel's sake, he found it again in the hearts of many who were led to Christ by his witness.

• • • •

THE GREAT WITNESS

Homer Rodeheaver used to tell this story of Joey:

> Joey was not very bright. He would never leave the tabernacle at night until he could shake my hand. He would stand right next to me until the last man had gone in order to say good-bye. It was embarrassing at times.

One night a man came forward to speak. He said, "I want to thank you for being so kind to Joey. He isn't quite bright, but he has never enjoyed anything so much as coming here and singing in the choir. He works hard during the day but wants to come to the services too. It is through him that my wife and my five children have been led to the Lord. His grandfather, seventy-five years old and an infidel all his life, and his grandmother have come tonight for salvation, and now the whole family is converted."

God has given you a place to witness, and you must not fail to do it. Joey is a good example.

You don't have to be highly educated to tell a lost person, "God loves you and wants to save you," and read him a few words from John's Gospel on how he can receive Christ.

••••

THE CONVERTED BURGLAR

What a joy to be a soul winner! This past week when I picked up a little book, I saw a story of a Mr. Lee, a minister in Waterford, New York.

It said that late one night while sitting in his study, he was startled to hear a strange noise behind him. Turning in his chair, he saw the grim face of a burglar. The man had entered the house by a side window, supposing that all were fast asleep. Pointing a pistol at the preacher's heart, he said, "Don't make any noise, or I'll shoot."

"You may put down your weapon, sir. I shall make no resistance," said the man of God. "You are at liberty to take all the valuables I possess. In fact, I will conduct you to the place where my most precious treasures are kept."

He got up and, opening the door, pointed into the other room. The burglar saw two cots on which Brother Lee's children were sleeping in youthful innocence.

"These," the preacher announced with affection, "are

my choicest jewels and treasures. Would you think of taking them?"

He then went on to say to the burglar that as a minister he had few earthly possessions and he had dedicated all his means to taking care of his two motherless children.

The burglar was deeply moved and expressed deep sorrow for the act that he had been about to commit. Brother Lee seized the opportunity to witness to the would-be criminal. Soon the intruder was kneeling beside him for prayer. Then in the silence of midnight the offender poured forth his remorse and penitence and received Christ as his Saviour. The pastor told him to go on his way, sin no more, and rejoice in the Lord.

Yes, the Lord will use various means to bring people to Himself. Let us be pliable in the Master's hands. Let us pray and keep ourselves ready to serve Him and to witness for Him.

••••

COURAGEOUS TO STAND!

Captain Hedley Vicars was a Christian hero of the Crimean War. The story about him is familiar to many.

On the morning after his conversion, he bought a large Bible and placed it open on the table of his room, determined that for the future an open Bible should be his "colors."

"It was to speak for me before I was strong enough to speak for myself," he said.

Captain Vicars' comrades laughed at him, telling him he would become a hypocrite. In spite of everything, Captain Vicars stood by his "colors." He became a strong spiritual power among army men simply by being a steadfast, bold, dedicated witness for Christ.

Be courageous to stand!

••••

A WIFE'S TESTIMONY PAYS OFF

This week I read the story of a woman who accepted Jesus as Saviour when she was a teenager. Later she married an unsaved man. This was a mistake, but she kept on living for Christ every day.

Years passed. Her husband cared nothing for Christ; he would not even attend church. The brokenhearted wife remained true to her Lord, living a deeply consecrated life. When children were born, the mother taught them to love Christ and to accept Him as Saviour.

Finally, disease hit her body. At the place of death, she called her husband to her bedside and said, "My dear, I have tried to be a faithful wife. I do hope that you will receive Christ as your Saviour and bring the little ones up in the right way. I have witnessed to you and sought to bring you to Him through these years. Up until now I have failed, but I am asking that you receive Him before I pass away so that someday you and the children will meet me in Heaven."

She called her children to her bedside and said to them, "I have taught you to look to Jesus. I have trained you to walk with Him. I hope you will always be faithful to the Lord."

After the funeral at the church, her body was taken to the cemetery for burial. The husband and children stood by and saw the last clod of earth fall on the casket. They went home with heavy hearts. It seemed that all the light had gone out of the sky for them.

That night the father put the children to bed and sat by the fireside thinking. Soon he heard the little boy sobbing. Going into the bedroom he asked, "What's the matter, Johnny? Are you hungry?"

"No sir," he answered.

"Are you thirsty?"

"No sir."

The father said, "What's the trouble, Son?"

The little boy said, "Papa, Mama used to get all of us around her knees at night and read to us about Jesus. Then she would put her hands on our heads and pray for us. You put us to bed without her prayers."

Later, when the father gave his testimony, he said, "I couldn't stand it any longer. I got the children up, read through some verses out of my wife's Bible, then I fell on my knees by the children and told God that I wanted Christ to be my Saviour, that I would give Him my heart and life right then, and that I wanted Him to use me to train my children for the Lord."

That man became a faithful Christian because of the constant testimony of a wife.

By that illustration I am trying to press upon your hearts the need for faithfulness and witnessing. What do you suppose those children would have become had their daddy not been saved after God had taken their "light" from the home?

••••

WHAT HAPPENED WHEN A FRIEND FAILED HIS FRIEND

Two businessmen lived on the outskirts of a city. One was saved; the other was unsaved.

One man went to his church every Sunday morning; the unsaved man never went to church. They came into the city from the suburbs every weekday morning on the same train. After work they would ride back home together in the evening.

It came about that at the same time both became ill. Each lay upon his dying bed. The unsaved man's wife, herself a Christian, was in such agony about him that she was constrained to say, "Husband, wouldn't you like for a good Christian to come and talk with you about Christ? You are very sick, and you may not live, and you are unsaved."

Her husband answered, "Not at all. My neighbor, Mr. _____, is a churchman, a Christian, he says; but in all these long years, we have ridden thousands of miles together, talked about every subject upon which men could converse, but never once has he said a word to me about religion. If there was anything to it, if it was important, surely he would have said something. Since he could pass by the subject all these years and be silent about it, I'll go away just as I am."

He died unsaved because a friend failed him.

•••••

TWO BROTHERS

There were two boys in the Taylor family. The older said he must make a name for the family, so he turned his face toward Parliament and fame. The younger decided to give his life to the service of Christ, so he turned his face toward China and duty.

Hudson Taylor, the missionary, died beloved and known on every continent. When I looked in the encyclopedia to see what the other son had done, I found these words: "The brother of Hudson Taylor."

The life that counts is the life given to Christ. May God help each Christian in this church to take a new look at himself and determine to give his best to Christ. It may not bring you fame, but it will bring you a reward as a soul winner.

•••••

HENRY HEINZ WON 267!

Someone asked Henry Heinz of the "57 Varieties" fame: "Since you are a Christian, why are you not up and at it?"

Heinz became very angry and went home to bed, but

sleep eluded him. At four o'clock in the morning, he prayed that God would make him a power in his work. Then he went to sleep.

At the next meeting of bank presidents he attended, Mr. Heinz turned to the man next to him and spoke of Christ. The man looked at him in amazement and said, "I wondered many times why, if you really believed in Christ, you had never spoken to me!"

From that time on, Henry Heinz kept busy leading others to Jesus Christ. The bank president was the first of 267 souls whom he was able to win.

Will you let the Lord use you?

••••

A WISE MAN'S ANSWER

Coleridge, a nineteenth-century English poet, was talking with a man who told him that he did not believe in giving little children any religious instruction whatsoever. His theory was that the child's mind should not be prejudiced in any direction. When he reached the years of discernment, he should be permitted to choose his own religious opinions.

Coleridge said nothing at that time. After awhile he asked his visitor if he would like to see his garden. When the man said he would, Coleridge took him out to the garden where only weeds were growing.

The man looked at Coleridge in surprise. "Why, this is not a garden! There is nothing here but weeds!"

"Well, you see," answered Coleridge, "I did not wish to infringe upon the liberty of the garden in any way. I was just giving the garden a chance to express itself and to choose its own production."

••••

"LET ME INTRODUCE YOU TO THE REAL PREACHER"

A famous preacher closed one of his powerful sermons with an earnest gospel appeal. A woman of wealth and social distinction hastened down the aisle and asked permission to say a few words to the audience. She said:

> I want you to know just why I came forward tonight. It was not by any word spoken by this good preacher. I stand here because of the little woman who sits before me. Her fingers are rough with toil. The hard work of many years has stooped her low. She is just a poor, obscure washerwoman who has served in our home for many years.
>
> I have never known her to be impatient, speak an unkind word, nor do a dishonorable deed. I know of countless little acts of unselfish love that adorn her life. Shamefully, let me say that I have openly sneered at her faith and laughed at her fidelity to God. Yet when my little girl was recently taken away, it was this woman who caused me to look beyond the grave and shed my first tear of hope. The sweet magnetism of her life has led me to Christ. I covet the thing that has made her life so beautiful.

The preacher was quite surprised. He asked the little woman to be led forward. She came with eyes filled with glad tears and with such a smiling face as one seldom sees on this side of Heaven.

The minister said, "Let me introduce you to the real preacher of this evening." The great, tearful audience arose spontaneously in silent respect.

"Let your light so shine before men, that they may see your good works, and glorify your Father which is in heaven."—Matt. 5:16.

This is what God wants of us—that we might be saved and filled with the Holy Spirit and faithfully witness day by day to others.

INDEX

Y

For a complete list of books available from the Sword of the Lord, write to Sword of the Lord Publishers, P. O. Box 1099, Murfreesboro, Tennessee 37133.

(800) 247-9673
(615) 893-6700
FAX (615) 848-6943
E-mail: 102657.3622@compuserve.com